WE
SHOULD
ALL BE
MIRANDAS

WE SHOULD ALL BE MIRANDAS

Life Lessons from *Sex and the City's* Most Underrated Character

CHELSEA FAIRLESS & LAUREN GARRONI
Illustrated by Carly Jean Andrews

HOUGHTON MIFFLIN HARCOURT
Boston   New York   2019

For information about permission to reproduce selections from this book,
write to trade.permissions@hmhco.com or to Permissions,
Houghton Mifflin Harcourt Publishing Company,
3 Park Avenue, 19th Floor, New York, New York 10016.

hmhbooks.com

Library of Congress Cataloging-in-Publication Data is available.
ISBN 978-0-358-02236-7

Illustrations by Carly Jean Andrews
Book design by Allison Chi

Printed in the United States of America
WOR 10 9 8 7 6 5 4 3 2 1

We Should All Be Mirandas provides life lessons inspired by a character from the
Sex and the City television series. It has not been created by the authors
or owners of that series, and has not been approved, sponsored, or endorsed
by the authors or owners of that series.

To every woman who has dared
to eat cake out of the garbage.

CONTENTS

Our Journey to Miranda

Hello, Lover!

Lauren and Chelsea here. We are the authors of this book, and we are both Mirandas. Chelsea is a Miranda with a Samantha rising and Lauren is a Miranda with a Carrie rising—but more on that later. Even though we are proud to identify as Mirandas today, the road to self-acceptance has been rough. When we first discovered *Sex and the City*, both of us felt a strong kinship with Carrie. She was the series' preeminent It girl, with a cool job, a hot sex life, and a plentiful supply of Nicolas Ghesquière-era Balenciaga. She was charismatic and impossibly chic, yet flawed enough to be relatable. In a matter of months, we were both self-proclaimed Carries, with the vintage slip dresses to prove it. Chelsea smoked Ms. Bradshaw's preferred brand of cigarettes (Marlboro Lights) before begrudgingly quitting, while Lauren almost broke up with her college boyfriend for merely *suggesting* that she was a Miranda. It's shameful to admit, but in the early aughts, *no one* wanted to be a Miranda—but we both had a change of heart when we revisited the series as adults. Miranda's take-no-shit attitude was inspiring. Her pantsuits were chicer than we remembered, and her mere presence was an essential counter to Carrie's drama and Charlotte's optimism. After repeat viewings, we started to question why we had aligned ourselves with Carrie at all, especially given her fondness for finance bros and fascinators.

We Should All Be Mirandas was born from our satirical Instagram account Every Outfit on Sex & the City (@everyoutfitonsatc), which launched in 2016 with a simple mission to document every outfit on the series. After conceiving of the account during a night of drinking, we began posting images of the show's more outrageous ensembles, accompanied by irreverent captions. Within days, it amassed tens of thousands of followers. We anticipated that our audience would enjoy revisiting Carrie's wacky fashion blunders—after all, her belt-over-a-bare-midriff look is just as batshit today as it was in 2002. But it quickly became apparent that Ms. Hobbes had an equally devoted (and chronically underserved) fan base. A post celebrating her overalls and puffer coat look from season two elicited such a strong response that we realized that there were a lot of other closeted Mirandas out there.

This revelation led us to question exactly *why* we had been so reluctant to identify with her in the first place. It quickly became apparent that we had been gaslit—by society, and the series itself—into believing that Miranda was the least aspirational character. Sure, she had her awkward moments, and yes, some of her hairstyles throughout the course of the show were truly bizarre. At the end of the day, though, this woman is a Harvard graduate who made partner by the age of thirty-five. She owns a brownstone and employs a full-time housekeeper. If that isn't aspirational, we don't know what is.

After we became aware of the societal bias against the Miranda-identified, we had to give it a name: Mirandaphobia. We delve into this concept on page 12, but in short, Mirandaphobia is the belief that Mirandas are inferior to other *Sex and the City* personality types. After internalizing this toxic messaging for most of our adult lives, we hid our true nature from our friends, our families, and (most importantly) ourselves. This resulted in some seriously self-destructive behavior, like romanticizing toxic love affairs and wearing stilettos in the dead of winter. We thought that adopting a Carrie-esque lifestyle would lead us down the path of enlightenment. Instead, we wound up with sociopathic lovers and a closet full of regrettable H&M purchases. However, after a considerable amount of soul-searching, we are proud to say that Miranda Hobbes is the only icon we need. Beyond her six-figure salary and designer wardrobe, Miranda's fierce intelligence and drama-free approach to living are the real things worth coveting. She speaks her mind, stands her ground, and refuses to apologize for her success—or the contents of her bedside drawer. Ms. Hobbes eschews repressive gender norms with style and grace, all while serving up the greatest menswear looks that you've ever seen. In short, we should all be Mirandas. To those of you who are out and proud, we salute you. As for those of you who are still closeted, we hope this helps.

—*Chelsea Fairless & Lauren Garroni*

CHAPTER 1

ARE YOU A MIRANDA?

The First Step Is Admitting
That You Are Not a Carrie

What Is a Miranda?

SHE'S MORE COMMON THAN YOU THINK

The women of *Sex and the City* aren't just characters—they're archetypes. There's the fashionable one, the traditional one, the hedonistic one, and the smart one who occasionally eats cake out of the garbage. Each woman's personality was distinct from the get-go, but it wasn't until HBO began selling t-shirts declaring "I'm a Carrie," "I'm a Charlotte," "I'm a Miranda," and "I'm a Samantha" that the public was forced to choose sides. Droves of eager tourists bought the shirts from HBO's flagship store in Times Square, inspiring a mini-backlash from locals who were tired of sharing their city with legions of overly enthusiastic *Sex and the City* fans. Despite the ridicule, these phrases quickly entered the cultural lexicon, inspiring millions of fans to self-identify as the characters. Most people identified with Carrie, the series' protagonist and widely considered to be the most enviable character. The more conservative fans gravitated toward Charlotte, feeling a kinship to her good-girl persona. The unabashedly promiscuous easily related to Samantha. And the people who would rather die than hear a grown man whisper "ever thine, ever mine, ever ours"—those would be Mirandas.

For better or worse, the Miranda personality type is typically characterized by a mild distrust of the world and the norms set upon it by society. Charlottes may label us as pessimists, but being a realist in an age of insanity has helped us to preserve what little dignity we have left. This go-to defense mechanism does not make us heartless, despite what our exes may shout as they leave. On the contrary, Mirandas love fiercely. We are very attentive in our friendships, occasionally at the expense of our own sanity. However, while Mirandas are loyal, we are not fools. So if your BFF needs to be reprimanded for gabbing about her relationship drama while you're suffering from a neck injury, so be it.

Autonomy in every facet of life is paramount for a Miranda. Being self-sufficient and living life authentically are essential for maintaining one's mental health. Mirandas put a great deal of time and effort into building their lives, so we are reluctant to let other people come in and fuck them up. Some may critique our cautious nature, but we're not afraid to take the mechanical bull by the horns if the situation calls for it. We are perfectly capable of adapting when life throws us a curveball, like an unplanned pregnancy or a relocation to Brooklyn. But while we may not be able to control everything in our lives (as micromanaging only goes so far), we know how to prepare for the worst. The key to a self-governed Miranda existence is prioritizing long-term goals over whims of instant gratification. While buying those Gucci loafers may feel good, being able to own a home is even better. If you're not there yet, don't fret. Mirandas are driven and resourceful people. We can accomplish anything with enough time, determination, and chlamydia medication.

The
Evolution
of
Miranda

Season 1 (1998)

Season 2 (1999)

Season 3 (2000)

It's been a fucking *journey*, but Miranda Hobbes's transition from the understated business attire of season one to the amped-up glamour of the *Sex and the City* films is the stuff of legend. Let her semi-awkward evolution inspire you on your own quest for sartorial fulfillment.

Season 4 (2002)   Season 6 (2004)   The First Film (2008)

A Day in the Life of a Miranda

6:00 a.m.   Alarm goes off. Press snooze.

6:10 a.m.   Press snooze again.

7:30 a.m.   Startle awake. You've pressed snooze so many times that now you can't go to the gym.

8:00 a.m.   Attempt to make a smoothie, before discovering that you don't have any bananas. Decide to get a doughnut on the way to work instead.

8:30 a.m.   Run into your ex on the street, causing you to spill coffee on your new blouse.

8:45 a.m.   Call your friend from Duane Reade, filling her in on your emotional mini-drama while searching for Tide pens.

9:30 a.m.   The meeting that you're in is pointless, so you do a deep dive of your nemesis's Instagram. Accidentally like a photo from eighteen months ago. Spend the next two hours in a panic spiral.

12:00 p.m.   Try and leave for lunch to take your mind off your social snafu, but get intercepted by work emails. Remain chained to your desk for hours.

3:00 p.m.   Inhale a prepackaged salad from Au Bon Pain.

4:30 p.m.   Start dreading the post-work cocktail with an acquaintance that you committed to ages ago. You canceled last time, so you're fucked.

5:00 p.m.	Fire your intern.
6:30 p.m.	Miraculously, your acquaintance cancels. You are free.
7:30 p.m.	Attend a nearby gallery opening because of the open bar. After spotting your nemesis across the room, you bolt.
8:15 p.m.	Arrive home, spend the next forty minutes deciding what to order from Grubhub. Pick the same Thai place you order from three times a week.
9:00 p.m.	Watch a television show about murder so you can finally relax.
10:00 p.m.	Shower, hopefully washing off the indignity of the day.
10:30 p.m.	Put on your mouthguard and attempt to sleep.
11:00 p.m.	Nowhere close to sleep, you grab your vibrator. Realizing it's not charged, read TMZ for thirty minutes until the light turns green.
11:40 p.m.	Squeeze out one perfunctory orgasm and toss the vibrator across the room.
12:00 a.m.	Finally drift off to sleep, hoping that you won't make the same mistakes tomorrow.

How to Spot a Miranda

Unless she is wearing a down jacket and a Yankees cap, you can't always identify a Miranda by her appearance alone. A Miranda can be any race, age, or size. We are as diverse as Samantha Jones's sexual partners. But while every Miranda is certainly unique, there are a handful of visual signifiers that can help you spot a fellow member of the sisterhood.

NO-MAKEUP MAKEUP A low-fuss, natural makeup look is a tell-tale sign of a Miranda. We tend to be minimalists when it comes to beauty, having developed a daily regimen of tinted moisturizer (the highest SPF available), blush, and tinted brow gel. However, it's worth noting that overworked Mirandas do have a tendency to go overboard with the undereye concealer. Watch out for that.

NO FRILLS You will never see a Miranda in an outfit that is excessively feminine. We may wear skirts and enjoy pastels, but we're not about to parade around the West Village in a tutu. Pearls, peplums, and peep-toes are to be avoided at all costs—that shit is for Charlottes.

clean face

baseball
hat

practical
outerwear

major
denim

nondescript
sneakers

ARE YOU A MIRANDA?

PRACTICAL FOOTWEAR A functional shoe is another typical signifier of a Miranda, although this is by no means a foolproof method of identification. Look for classic sneakers, loafers, slides, and other comfort-centric footwear.

SHORT HAIR Not all Mirandas have short hair, but a disproportionate percentage of women with this hairstyle identify as Mirandas. The minimal upkeep appeals to our no-nonsense nature—after all, who has time for blow-outs?

MIRANDA BY ASSOCIATION See that girl at the gym in a Tori Amos t-shirt? She's a Miranda. Or that woman in a coffee shop with a PBS tote bag? Also a Miranda. The quickest way to identify a Miranda is through merch—specifically merch from cultural institutions, bookstores, podcasts, and liberal media outlets.

"

I drink coffee, have sex, buy pies, and enjoy battery-operated devices.

"

Mirandaphobia

There is a reason that you've been reluctant to self-identify as a Miranda for so long, and it has a name: Mirandaphobia. Simply put, Mirandaphobia is the institutionalized belief that Mirandas are inferior to the Carries, Charlottes, and Samanthas of the world. This toxic rhetoric has permeated our culture since the advent of *Sex and the City*, resulting in many Mirandas choosing to remain closeted. They have internalized intense feelings of shame, often to the detriment of their own self-worth and their relationships with others. Our Carrie-normative culture has perpetuated the myth that embodying the characteristics of a Miranda (blunt, sarcastic, career-focused) are undesirable qualities for a woman.

It's textbook sexism, and it doesn't take a genius to realize that our oppression only benefits the patriarchy. But before we attempt to eradicate Mirandaphobia on a global scale, we must first examine our own inner bias.

Do you find yourself lashing out when you're referred to as the Miranda of the group? This misplaced aggression is the first sign of Mirandaphobia. Mirandas have been conditioned to feel inferior, and continuing to hold on to this belief only makes us complicit in our own marginalization. Unpacking these unpleasant emotions is the first step to overcoming Mirandaphobia. And if you're holding this book in your hands, you're well on your way.

Major pantsuits

Incredibly loyal

Righteously opinionated

Accepts that he's just not that into you

Not here for Carrie's bullshit

Devotee of baked goods

Always sarcastic

Famous Mirandas in History

Being a career-minded pragmatist who refuses to put up with bullshit is not unique to Miranda Hobbes. She is part of a lineage of highly intelligent, forward-thinking women who spurned expected gender roles in order to forge their own paths to success. Despite their legions of detractors, these strong-willed women pushed the culture forward *and* popularized pantsuits in the process. Without their pioneering efforts, we could not live openly as Mirandas today.

JOAN OF ARC, *Saint* (1412–1431) While most Miranda-identified individuals would roll their eyes at Joan of Arc for believing that God had chosen her to save France, we must respect her heroine status. Born Jeanne d'Arc, Joan lived on her parents' farm until visions compelled her to lead the French Army to victory against the English at Orléans. She was captured a year later and put on trial for heresy, witchcraft, and dressing like a man. Joan's refusal to wear women's clothing while jailed—a countermeasure to being raped—led the court to believe she was a heretic and therefore was sentenced to burned at the stake. She died a martyr and an icon to androgyny.

HILLARY RODHAM CLINTON, *Politician* (1947–) Is there any doubt that Hillary is a Miranda? From her love of suits to her Ivy League law degree, these women are two sides of the same coin. Throughout her prolific career, Clinton has lost almost as much as she has succeeded—and all on a very public stage. Despite her fumbles, she has always moved forward with grace and purpose. Critics can fuss about her likability all they want, but we will always carry the torch for this boundary-breaking icon.

ROXANE GAY, *Writer* (1974–) Roxane Gay has a *lot* of opinions. From her landmark essay collection *Bad Feminist* to her utterly essential Twitter feed, Gay has become the preeminent cultural critic for the Miranda-identified. She is a best-selling novelist, a *New York Times* contributor, and a pop culture obsessive who examines lowbrow and highbrow culture with equal reverence. Gay reminds us that standing up and using your voice is absolutely crucial for the Miranda-identified.

KATHARINE HEPBURN, *Actress* (1907–2003) An outlier in her chosen profession, Katharine Hepburn personified the modern independent woman way before it was de rigueur. She built a career playing intelligent and fiercely independent characters—and, later in life, chic spinsters. On- and offscreen, her persona defied the patriarchal ideals of womanhood. Hepburn was outspoken, never had children, and carried on a two-decade-long affair with the married Spencer Tracy. We also have her to thank for bringing trousers into the mainstream.

REI KAWAKUBO, *Fashion Designer* (1942–) Despite her lack of any formal fashion training, Rei Kawakubo created one of the most influential brands in the world. After stints in advertising and styling, Kawakubo began designing clothes under the label Comme des Garçons in 1969. Nearly five decades later, she is the reigning queen of the avant-garde. Her outré, genre-defying clothing has garnered a massive cult following and near-universal praise from fashion critics. In 2017, she achieved the rare distinction of being the first living female designer to receive a solo show at The Met's Costume Institute. Although extremely private, Kawakubo is instantly recognizable by her chic blunt bob and biker jacket.

FRAN LEBOWITZ, *Writer* (1950–) Armed with her acerbic wit and Savile Row wardrobe, Fran Lebowitz made a career out of her sardonic dissections of New York life. In the early seventies, she penned a column for *Interview* magazine before going on to achieve literary success with her seminal essay collections *Metropolitan Life* and *Social Studies*. Her status as Manhattan's preeminent cultural critic and style icon has remained unchanged for over four decades, as has her signature coif.

CONSTANCE BAKER MOTLEY, *Judge* (1921–2005) The prolific and badass Constance Baker Motley paved the way for African American women in law. After graduating from Columbia Law School, Motley was the first female attorney hired by the NAACP. During the fifties and sixties, she had a hand in almost every significant civil rights case, winning nine out of the ten cases that she argued in front of the Supreme Court. However, she is best known for being the first African American female federal judge, a position she held for nearly forty years.

HONORABLE MENTIONS

Diane Keaton • Whoopi Goldberg • Lee Israel • Grace Coddington
Angela Davis • Ruth Bader Ginsburg • Annie Lennox • Virginia Woolf
Condoleezza Rice • Joan Didion • Dorothy Parker • Jodie Foster
Greta Garbo • Bea Arthur • Gloria E. Anzaldúa • Molly Ringwald
Miuccia Prada • Eleanor Roosevelt • Lisa Simpson • Leslie Feinberg
Audre Lorde • Isabella Rossellini • Janeane Garofalo • Tori Amos
Grace Lee Boggs • The Wachowskis • Marie Curie • Urvashi Vaid
Amelia Earhart • Chelsea Manning • Rachel Dratch • Isabelle
Huppert • Lynne Ramsay • Gertrude Stein • Jil Sander • Tilda
Swinton • Rachel Maddow • Issa Rae • Daria Morgendorffer
Susan Sontag • Hedy Lamarr • Annemarie Schwarzenbach
Billie Jean King • Judith Butler • Jenna Wortham • Gayatri Spivak
Elizabeth Warren • Robyn Ochs

10 Signs That
You Are a Miranda

1. Unplugging is your idea of hell.

2. You're not a girly girl.

3. You've had more regrettable sex than you care to remember.

4. You have your shit together—for the most part.

5. You hate baby showers.

6. Your bad hair days are legendary.

7. You have a housekeeper named Magda.

8. You turn to baked goods in times of crisis.

9. You have a notorious tabloid addiction.

10. What you lack in sex appeal, you make up for in personality.

I've Never Had an Opinion in My Life

THE MIRANDA'S GUIDE TO WHAT'S HOT AND WHAT'S NOT

Mirandas are not indifferent people. We either love something or we hate it, and everyone in our vicinity is keenly aware of our hot takes on everything from Prada to pubic hair. If Carries thrive on shopping sprees, we thrive via defending our own well-researched, iron-clad convictions. But while preferences within the sisterhood may vary slightly, there are certain things that all Mirandas can agree upon.

HOT	NOT
BBC dramas	ceramic frogs
Daily Mail	spray tans
The New York Yankees	maximalism
Balenciaga	other people's children
therapy	tulle
pinstripes	camping
marathons	ghosts
Tevas	Tomi Lahren
Barneys	bedskirts
podcasts	Mr. Big
Dr. Robert Leeds	sexual harassment
fried chicken	contouring
Clinique "Black Honey" lipstick	cold shoulder dresses
The Container Store	cheating
Ketel One	logomania
turtlenecks	tea sandwiches
historical biographies	life coaches
Uniqlo	mules
judging others	gender reveal parties
naps	Frappuccinos
Postmates	Facebook
sweetgreen	fillers
Joan Didion	Yeezy
Spanx	Louis C.K.
Harvard	Balmain
documentaries	#MondayMotivation

What Kind of
Miranda Are You?

Being a Miranda does not preclude you from relating to other characters on the show. We'll be the first to admit that almost everyone has a little bit of Carrie in them. Many Mirandas are promiscuous like Samantha, while others are closet traditionalists like Charlotte. Some Mirandas even present as other characters, although this is often the result of internalized Mirandaphobia. Whatever the case, your rising sign is an integral part of who you are and how the world sees you. If you don't already know what your ascendant sign is, we've included a handy flow chart on pages 24–25 for your convenience.

What Kind of Miranda Are You?

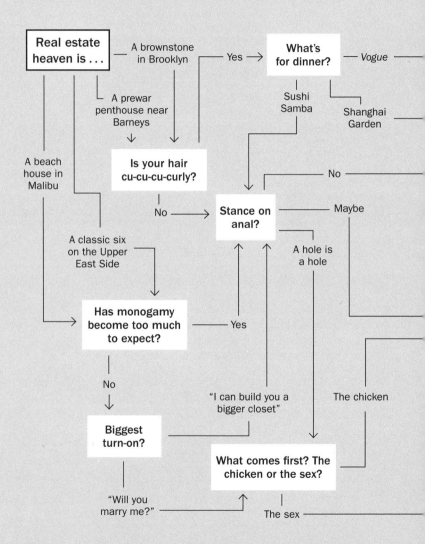

Real estate heaven is . . .

A brownstone in Brooklyn

A prewar penthouse near Barneys

A beach house in Malibu

Is your hair cu-cu-cu-curly?

No

A classic six on the Upper East Side

Has monogamy become too much to expect?

Yes

No

Biggest turn-on?

"Will you marry me?"

Yes → **What's for dinner?** — *Vogue*

Sushi Samba

Shanghai Garden

No

Stance on anal? — Maybe

A hole is a hole

"I can build you a bigger closet"

The chicken

What comes first? The chicken or the sex?

The sex

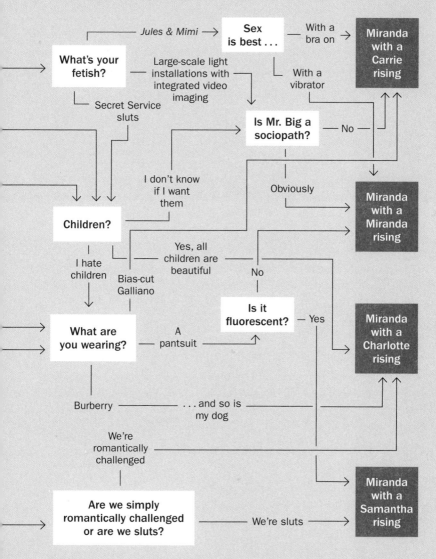

ARE YOU A MIRANDA?

Miranda with a Carrie Rising

You may have your shit together, but you also have an oven filled with shoes. Mirandas with a Carrie rising are constantly at odds with themselves, attempting to reconcile the pragmatic and romantic sides of their brains. This personality type is cursed with knowing what the right choice is, but habitually making the wrong one anyway. They might pay off their student loans one month, but spend their entire savings on a vintage caftan the next.

Carefully cultivating a "look" is both an act of control and a pre-ferred form of cardio. They are creative people by nature and will often channel those impulses into side hustles, which can provide them with a bit of a cushion should their building go co-op. Like all Mirandas, they are full of opinions, delivering sardonic quips on everything from politics to this year's Met Gala theme. But while they are eager to assert themselves, they are also extremely sensitive, which puts them at an emotional disadvantage when criticism is leveled.

Despite their precarious nature, they are routinely the go-to resource for unbiased advice among their friends. Proceed with caution, though. Mirandas with a Carrie rising are not known for taking their own advice, frequently to the point of self-destruction. Food and fashion are often crutches in times of conflict, but others rarely view them as vices because your taste in both is impeccable. You are a closet hedonist, hence the eating cake out of the garbage, but you will always look fabulous while doing it.

Miranda with a Samantha Rising

Screw convention—that soul-sucking trap is for Charlottes. Your primary aim in life is to achieve happiness and personal fulfillment through your social life and your career. You don't need to be married. You don't need—or want—children. You don't even need a partner to have mind-blowing orgasms, because that's what your Sharper Image neck massager is for. Mirandas with a Samantha rising are highly driven and self-sufficient people. They are deeply opinionated and confident in their convictions, which often deviate from the status quo. They carve their own paths in life, and tend to avoid people who conform to societal norms.

They also like sex—a lot. Having a diverse and fulfilling sex life is a *requirement* for a Miranda with a Samantha rising, not an option. Their happiness and sense of well-being depend on it. When they lack an adequate sexual outlet, they tend to lash out at those around them.

Apart from the occasional bout of sexual frustration, this personality type is generally even-tempered and dependable. But even though Mirandas with a Samantha rising have high tolerances for other people's bullshit, they do have their limits. Sometimes you need to avoid unnecessary drama at all costs, even if it means disinviting the entire crew from your dinner at Samba.

Miranda with a Charlotte Rising

It hardly seems possible, but yet here you are, existing at the nexus of hopeless cynicism and profound optimism. Your number one goal is to have a perfect life, and to get to that perfect life as quickly and painlessly as possible. The future you desire has been culled from the sappy romance novels and paperback erotica that you read secretly in your teen years (and let's be honest, you're still reading that trash). Guilt is a hallmark of this personality type, as is the warmer, fuzzier offshoot of guilty pleasure.

Despite your somewhat conservative presentation, you are surprisingly down for majorly transgressive sex. Threesomes, cross-dressing, and anilingus may repulse you initially, but at some point, you'll probably wind up fellating someone in a dark alley. But while your sexual tastes may be eccentric, you are a ride-or-die basic bitch at your core. You love *Love Actually,* pumpkin spice lattes, and impromptu Target runs. You are a stickler for the rules, but that's not to say you're a pushover. When you see injustice, you call it out passionately. This personality type can solve anything with their can-do attitude—apart from curing their partner's erectile dysfunction, that is.

Miranda with a Miranda Rising

Holy shit, you're as Miranda as it gets. We wouldn't be surprised if you were wearing adult braces *right now*—which isn't a critique, by the way. To the contrary, we are simply acknowledging that Mirandas with a Miranda rising have to deal with a lot of bullshit. You may have advantages in life, but you tend to attract bad dates and bad hair days with a higher frequency than most.

Those minor mishaps aside, there are several advantages to being a Miranda through and through. For one, you are completely self-sufficient. You don't depend on others to take care of you, because you always rely on yourself. And it should come as no surprise that the most prominent characteristic of Mirandas with Miranda rising is their deeply opinionated natures. Mirandas are not shy when it comes to speaking their minds, whether it be about their friends' pretentious boyfriends or the current Yankees lineup. This would be a far less attractive quality if not for the fact that they are almost always right.

<u>WHAT YOU SHOULD HAVE</u>
<u>LEARNED FROM THIS CHAPTER</u>

- Accept that you are a Miranda.
- Examine your internalized Mirandaphobia.
- Sarcasm is a coping mechanism.
- You too can be a Miranda who makes history.
- Not all Mirandas wear overalls . . .
- . . . but many have short hair.
- To survive, you must know your rising sign.
- You are your opinions.
- Never apologize for who you are.
- You will never be an It girl—and that's okay.

CHAPTER 2

DRESS LIKE A MIRANDA

How to Layer a Bucket Hat
over a Hoodie and Other Lessons
from the Queen of Off-Duty

Miranda Hobbes,
Fashion Superstar

AN UNDERRATED ICON GETS HER DUE

After spending twenty years in the shadow of television's preeminent It girl, Miranda Hobbes has finally reached style-icon status. The fashion pendulum has swung, and puffer jackets, boxy suits, and Harvard hoodies are decidedly "in." When *Sex and the City* first aired, though, Ms. Hobbes's hypercorporate style went largely unnoticed. But just because she didn't have the wherewithal to wear a man's shirt as a dress doesn't mean that she lacked style. Although conservative, Miranda's wardrobe was distinctly androgynous, setting her apart from other archetypal "working women" on television. That (and her flame-red hair) gave her an instantly recognizable look that has stood the test of time.

Her penchant for oversize, nondescript clothing has also aged well, anticipating trends in both high fashion and streetwear. But despite her chicer moments, Miranda's wardrobe was designed to position her as the show's everywoman, not the ingenue. Sweatshirts, tote bags, and flat sandals were all off-duty staples. Unglamorous loungewear was abundant, while Samantha-esque lingerie was scant. Unlike her cohorts, Miranda was subjected to a host of horrors including (but not limited to) a neck brace, adult braces, and an entire season of lackluster postpartum looks. Throughout the series, Ms. Hobbes's mere presence was a reminder that the show was based in reality. Even after she reemerged as a couture-clad glamazon in the first *Sex and the City* film, audiences knew that the real Miranda was the makeup-free woman in gym clothes.

In recent years, the fashion world has finally caught up with Miranda's comfort-based, office-focused aesthetic. She has unwittingly become the patron saint of normcore, a youth-driven stylistic movement that recalls the unpretentious, mass-market clothing of the Y2K era. Several luxury brands have embraced this ethos, most notably Balenciaga, whose runway shows feature bare-faced, puffer jacket–clad models who could easily be mistaken for Ms. Hobbes. Her early-series staples like dad hats, sweatpants, and oversize blazers can now be purchased at Barneys. Echoes of her gender-bending business attire can be seen in recent collections from female-focused designers like Phoebe Philo and Victoria Beckham. But just because you personally identify with Miranda does not mean that you have to adopt her signature look, however fabulous. No one is forcing you to wear turtlenecks and Tevas. Dressing like a Miranda means sharing her attitude and outlook, not necessarily her penchant for track pants.

Not all Mirandas are fashionistas, but that doesn't mean that we lack style. Some of us live for clothes, while others give fewer fucks than Steve's mom. But no matter where you fall on the clotheshorse spectrum, every Miranda has a basic understanding of what kind of clothes suit her. If you can't figure this out on your own, find a Carrie-identified friend to assist you, and if all else fails, look to the classics: bootcut jeans, trench coats, and white t-shirts are timeless pieces that every Miranda can fall back on. What you *don't* want to do is let trends dictate your look. Resist the fast-fashion rat race at all costs, and instead focus on quality pieces that you can wear again and again.

If you constantly feel like you have nothing to wear or routinely suffer from outfit-related meltdowns, you are not buying the right clothes. You are also probably buckling under the soul-crushing societal pressure to look attractive at all times. No judgment— we've all fallen into this trap at one point or another. Dressing for the male gaze is *never* a good look for our people, so attempt to unlearn these toxic thinking patterns immediately. Mirandas aren't meant to be tamed, and we sure as hell aren't meant to wear body-con dresses. Find a look that makes *you* feel sexy and confident, even if that look involves a giant pair of overalls.

Executive Realness

Dressing for the workplace is all about maintaining the illusion that you are a dependable, upstanding member of society who would never get oral in the back of a taxicab. For Miranda Hobbes, dressing the part of a take-no-shit corporate lawyer was a necessity of her profession. Whereas Carrie could work barefoot in a Depression-era negligee, Miranda had to look polished and put-together at all times. With her starched collar and her pressed slacks, she exuded a distinctive Midtown vibe that her cohorts did not. Even if you don't have an office job, though, there are lessons to be learned from this hyper-regimented approach to workplace dressing.

While suits may feel oppressive to some, others find them liberating. Classic menswear styles have evolved to a point of perfection, so you can bypass the bullshit that comes with cycling through trends. Mixing and matching separates is also shockingly easy when all of your clothes are designed to match. The key is sticking to timeless, minimal pieces that are devoid of unnecessary embellishments. Your inner Carrie may urge you to buy a blazer with neon lining or epaulettes, but just remember that those superfluous

design elements are bound to look dated. Stick with classic silhouettes and good fabrics, and never, *ever* skimp on tailoring.

If suits aren't your thing, then establishing a personal uniform is absolutely crucial. Mirandas don't always have the time (or the ability) to craft a killer ensemble on the fly. Having a foolproof look that you can depend on in times of chaos will save you time *and* ward off sartorial breakdowns, so when you find something that you feel comfortable in, *replicate it.* Buy five oversize men's shirts, or pencil skirts, or whatever works for you. The aim is to slowly build a wardrobe of interchangeable separates that you can put together without thought or effort. Andy Warhol did it, Diana Vreeland did it, and noted Miranda Fran Lebowitz is living proof that people with uniforms are infinitely more chic than trend-chasers. Take a cue from the greats, and find a look for the workplace that you can stick to. You'll look like you have your shit together and maintain your sanity in the process.

Accessorize Like a Miranda

Some women accessorize with Birkins; others prefer exposed bras and Marlboro Lights. But Mirandas tend to gravitate toward pieces that actually make their lives easier. This could be a baseball cap that shields your face from the horrors of sun damage or a plastic shopping bag that transports your trashy tabloids from Point A to Point B. However, your pragmatism does not disqualify you from the occasional bout of Carrie-esque frivolity. Overpriced cocktails and handbags that cost more than your rent are acceptable indulgences as long as they occur infrequently. So with that in mind, here are the key pieces that every Miranda needs to own.

Jackie O Glasses
Jackie O was a Charlotte, but her
namesake sunglasses look fabulous
on Mirandas too. Case in point:
Kurt Cobain.

Bucket Hat
The most iconic Miranda Hobbes
accessory of all. Bonus points if you
style it over a hooded windbreaker.

Harvard Class of '90 Mug
As the Olsen Twins taught us, a
cup of coffee is one of the best
accessories there is.

Duane Reade Bag
Nothing says "I'm a real
New Yorker" quite like a modest
plastic shopping bag from this
ubiquitous drugstore chain.

Waist Belt
Mirandas strive to create
structure in their daily lives,
which is exactly what a good
belt does for your outfit.
Noted Miranda Diane Keaton
also swears by them.

Neck Brace
If you happen to require one
of these oppressive pieces of
foam at some point in your life,
congratulations. You've reached
the highest echelon of
Miranda-ness.

Bank Account–Obliterating Stilettos
You can (and should) buy those
obscenely expensive, wildly
impractical heels that you've been
lusting over. Just make sure to keep
a spare pair of flats on hand for the
trek home at 2:00 a.m.

Briefcase
Let those bitches know that you mean
business with a classic, understated
briefcase. Monogram it for a Charlotte-
esque touch of personalization.

"

I'm wearing a new dress from Barneys and I'm eating out of plastic.

"

Carrie's Fashion Corner

She may be grating at times, but Carrie's status as *Sex and the City*'s preeminent Fashion Goddess is indisputable. All those years of buying *Vogue* instead of dinner must have really paid off, because few women are able to cultivate such ironclad styling instincts. And while the average Miranda may not have the time (or the financial resources) to spend an entire afternoon looking for the perfect $7 vintage dress to go with a pair of $300 shoes, we can all learn something from her masterful, madcap approach to getting dressed.

1. **SHOPPING IS A FULL-TIME JOB** Visiting shops that you love on a near-constant basis is imperative to maintaining your look because you can never, ever find what you need when you are looking for it. For example, if you're looking for a trench coat, you will find an ostrich bolero instead. If you are looking for a sensible pair of walking shoes, you will find the skyscraper heels of your dreams. Conversely, when you aren't looking for anything, fabulous clothing is shockingly abundant. In short, you can't find the wardrobe that you need without putting in a steady, prolonged effort.

2. **FIND YOUR CARRIE NECKLACE** Any seasoned fashionista will tell you that having a go-to piece of jewelry or a signature accessory instantly personalizes your look. Carrie had her nameplate necklace, the strappy sandals, and the ever-present giant rosette. Get out there and find *your* giant rosette.

3. **MAKE TRENDS YOUR BITCH** Indulging in trends is very Carrie-esque, but letting them dictate your style is not. She was able to successfully participate in the trend cycle because her own fashion persona was so clearly defined that she never lost her identity to the latest, hottest thing. First discover your stylistic comfort zone, then stick to the trends that relate to it each season.

4. **BUY VINTAGE** Vintage shopping isn't just a hobby, it's a full-fledged lifestyle. It's one that Mirandas should seriously consider adopting. For one, it provides you with access to clothes that no one else has, perhaps the biggest luxury conceivable in today's overexposed fashion landscape. It also enables you to opt out of the fast-fashion cycle, which negatively impacts the planet and the scores of underpaid laborers that it relies upon.

5. **DON'T DRESS LIKE CARRIE** This is the most important rule. You can certainly draw inspiration from Carrie's genre-defying fashion sense, but attempting to replicate her signature brand of thrown-togetherness is never a good idea. Some people can wear a marching band jacket with a tulle petticoat and not look totally fucking insane—but Mirandas are not those people. Know thyself.

Tote Bags

Mirandas aren't hoarders by nature, but they have a tendency to accrue a freakish number of canvas tote bags. This is because totes encapsulate two qualities that Mirandas value immensely: practicality and affordability. Totes hold groceries, gym clothes, and your dog-eared copy of *He's Just Not That Into You* while simultaneously signifying your allegiance to NPR, Whole Foods, or your local independent bookstore. Because they are so cheap and readily available, we are constantly acquiring more. This is also due to the fact that tote bags get soiled and misshapen quickly—especially the cheap ones. But do we get rid of them? No. Instead, we pick a designated tote bag and we use that bag to store all of our old bags. It's not logical, but it's the Miranda way.

Loungewear
Looks

HOW TO DRESS FOR TAKE-OUT AND TIVO

There are two separate and distinct approaches to indoor dressing. The first is all about building a beautiful, comfort-focused lounge-wear wardrobe over time. This could include basics like leggings and nightshirts or more outré pieces like monogrammed slippers and dressing gowns. The second approach involves throwing on whatever ratty piece of garbage you can find on the floor at the end of a long, hard day. This approach emphasizes wearing clothes that look like shit but provide you with an optimal level of comfort when you're watching Rachel Maddow. Neither is wrong, and Ms. Hobbes certainly vacillated between both camps—but it's safe to say the majority of us are eating lo mein in unflattering sweatpants, and that's okay.

The biggest perk of dressing like a slob is having a short window of time in which you can detach from your own vanity. For many women, maintaining one's appearance requires an extraordinary amount of time, money, and unspoken emotional labor. Having the opportunity to disengage from the vicious cycle of personal grooming can be oddly therapeutic. However, there is *one* line that a completely out-of-fucks Miranda should never cross: wearing clothing that has been retired from your everyday wardrobe due to holes or stains. Your loungewear collection doesn't have to be fancy, but it shouldn't be a halfway house between your closet and the garbage can. You can wear all the mismatched pajamas you want, but that Merlot-stained Hanson t-shirt from 1995 has got to go.

Make Miranda
Androgynous Again

Miranda Hobbes's gender-bending fashion sense was never directly addressed on *Sex and the City,* but its audience certainly noticed. After all, her early series looks had more in common with Thin White Duke–era David Bowie than the hyperfeminine styles of her three cohorts. But beyond the slouchy suits and loafers, her short hair was the thing that pushed her look squarely into androgynous territory. Straight women rarely go butch from head to toe—apart from noted Miranda Annie Lennox. And unlike the Power Lesbians, who favored similar menswear styles in season two, Ms. Hobbes's atypical presentation was informed by her occupation, not her sexuality or gender identity. She spent her days in the stifling, male-dominated field of corporate law, where she presumably had to conform to their archaic dress codes. Sometimes she even accessorized with a straight tie, which ultimately looked more queer than corporate. However, as the series progressed, Miranda's business attire was gradually replaced with traditionally feminine clothing. By the time the squad got to Abu Dhabi, she too was teetering around in cocktail dresses and six-inch Louboutins. Despite her heteronormative makeover, we will always be partial to Miranda's original fashion persona.

The Miranda's Guide
to Sneakers

NOT ALL ICONS WEAR HEELS

Mirandas are purists when it comes to athletic foot-wear. They tend to favor classic, nondescript styles that can be procured at any Foot Locker, not the Kanye-approved drops. For the Miranda-identified, wearing sneakers is less about making a fashion statement and more about sating the desire for comfort. Athletic shoes enable us to walk freely in the world, unburdened by the bullshit that comes with wearing heels. Stilettos have a time and a place, of course, but a seasoned Miranda will always have a pair of Keds lurking in her handbag in case disaster strikes.

Keds Champion

ASICS GEL-Contend 3

adidas Superstar

New Balance 574

Nike Classic Cortez

Reebok Princess

WE SHOULD ALL BE MIRANDAS

Miranda Off-Duty

Mirandas have two full-time jobs: earning a living and looking presentable. We really should be paid for both, because putting together appropriate outfits for work, dates, and other social functions is *exhausting.* It requires our time, our energy, and far too many trips to the dry cleaner. So when we find ourselves in a situation where we aren't required to look polished, we embrace it. Oversize hoodies, leggings, and sneakers may not land us on the best-dressed list, but sometimes comfort is the ultimate luxury. Athleisure is having a moment, but we believe that a stylish outfit should happen by accident, not by design. Ease and function should be your top priorities, not getting papped by a street style photographer. This isn't to say that we should be roaming the streets looking like slobs—ikat pants and Tevas are as comfortable as they are chic. Dressing down in your off-hours is restorative—not only for your mental health, but also for your feet, which spend countless hours trapped in heels. Yes, you may run into an ex or frenemy when you feel less than glamorous, but if *Sex and the City* has taught us anything, it's that you can always hide behind a telephone pole in the event of a crisis.

Dressing to Get Laid

To put it bluntly, Mirandas are not known for getting their tits out. In the bedroom, yes. In the streets, no. Unlike Samanthas, they have little interest in dressing provocatively. This isn't about prudishness, or because they're ashamed of their bodies—although many of us have certainly fallen into that trap. It's because our people have zero desire to express their sexuality via a micro-mini dress. This isn't meant to shade the Versace-lovers of the world or suggest that women who wear revealing clothing are inferior in any way. It's just not how the Miranda-identified typically roll. They tend to rely on charm and intellect to attract lovers, not hemlines. Even though Mirandas may be gorgeous or chic or both of those things (see: Tilda Swinton), they don't typically *ooze* raw sexuality—at least not until they've had a few cocktails. Unfortunately, the problem with your lack of oozing is this: *you have to get laid*. Of course you don't need a slutty[1] outfit to attract a sexual partner. You've probably done it dozens of times *without* the aid of leather shorts. It's just that sometimes "putting it all out there" can be more efficient than burying your assets underneath "witty banter and little looks," as Ms. Hobbes laments in season three.

---

1   When we say "slutty," we mean it in the sex-positive, third-wave sense.

There is no single rule for semi-whorish[2] date-night dressing. Everyone's style should be derived from their own fashion ethos. Imagine Charlotte wearing one of Samantha's Crayola-colored Thierry Mugler power suits . . . okay, that sounds amazing, but you get the idea. It's about finding what works for you. Dressing to get laid is about working with what you have, not making up for what you don't. It's equally important to maintain a sense of authenticity during your slutty transformation. We're certainly not suggesting that you completely ignore your instincts, but it's important to occasionally wear something *slightly* sluttier than you would normally go for. If you need assistance, find a Samantha-identified friend to take you shopping when you're on the prowl.

---

2 Ditto. For the love of God, do not tweet at us.

The Life-Changing Magic of Throwing Out Shit You Don't Wear

Few will admit it, but closet-purging is an emotional minefield that most of us would rather avoid. If it weren't so difficult, you wouldn't have a wide selection of ill-fitting, ancient, or unworn garments hanging in your closet right now. Editing one's closet requires a person to take stock of all of their bad choices, whether it was wasting money on a piece that you never wore or indulging in a regrettable trend that you would prefer to forget. Closet-purging also requires a person to revisit their past, and all of the uncomfortable feelings that come along with that. Some people hoard clothes from their youth with sentimental value, willfully ignoring the fact that they will never wear platforms again. Others are forced to confront fluctuations in their weight, which can be insanely triggering for Mirandas with body image issues. Then there are the pieces that we hold on to even though they make us miserable. For example, after Mr. Big literally *left her at the altar,* Carrie was unable to part with her Vivienne Westwood wedding dress. She decided to keep it in a storage unit, where she no doubt avoided it for the rest of her natural life. This is the sort of toxic nostalgia that Mirandas must avoid *at all costs*. Hanging on to pieces that are imbued with misery will only make you miserable. There are no exceptions—not even for couture.

The only way to manage your wardrobe is to face your demons *head-on*. Only you can take the initiative to start this process, but by no means should you do it alone. If there's one thing that we learned from the first *Sex and the City* film (apart from the fact that Mr. Big is evil), it's that editing your closet is much more enjoyable when friends and alcohol are involved. Having assistance from someone who is not emotionally invested in your wardrobe will help you to look past your irrational reasons for keeping clothes that you never wear. But *who* you invite to your wardrobe editing soiree is key. There are two essential requirements: 1. the friend (or friends) must have good taste, and 2. they must be assertive enough to tell you that your clothes are ugly *to your face.* This is not a task for overly polite and sentimental Charlottes. A real closet purge requires another Miranda, or ideally a Samantha, who is blunt and bitchy enough to tell you the cold, hard truth.

Once you've assembled your support network and popped a bottle of Veuve Clicquot, you must go through every single item in your closet and ask yourself the following questions:

1. **DOES IT MAKE YOU HAPPY?**
2. **HAS IT SEEN BETTER DAYS?**
3. **DOES IT FIT?**
4. **IS IT WORTH ALTERING?**
5. **HAVE YOU WORN IT WITHIN THE LAST YEAR?**

Remember, this is a time for complete and utter ruthlessness. Getting rid of shit you don't wear will free up closet space that you desperately need *and* unburden you from the bad juju that comes with hoarding unused, emotionally loaded possessions. It may be challenging to let go of certain items in the moment, but remember that once you discard something that you truly do not need, you are unlikely to think about it ever again. More importantly, you'll make space for new, exciting things to come into your life. No single item can compete with the peace that comes with having an organized, functional wardrobe. Ditch those oppressive skinny jeans immediately—a whole new you is on the horizon.

WHAT YOU SHOULD HAVE LEARNED FROM THIS CHAPTER

- Establish a uniform.
- Androgyny isn't just for lesbians.
- Don't dress like Carrie.
- A neck brace can be fashionable.
- Buy shoes that you can walk in.
- Invest in good loungewear.
- Stop buying so many tote bags.
- Your emotional baggage is hanging in your closet.
- Resisting trends requires discipline.
- Look like you have your shit together, even if you don't.

CHAPTER 3

LOVE LIKE A MIRANDA

The Pessimist's Guide
to Happily Ever After

Love's a Bitch

. . . BUT SO ARE YOU

Contrary to popular belief, Mirandas desire love and romance just as much as your average Charlotte—we just don't broadcast it. Public displays of sentimentality are unnerving, especially impromptu piano ballads by Russian conceptual artists. Teddy bears, sky writing, and giant cookies that say "I Love You" do not move us. You will not catch us putting a bird on our head or waltzing in the streets of Manhattan anytime soon. Mirandas (and Samanthas) have the good sense to know that overly performative declarations of love are basic, especially in the age of social media. But while we resent having to witness our acquaintances' love lives unfolding online, we do have a soft spot for more practical expressions of love. Aidan's offer to single-handedly renovate Carrie's apartment was perhaps the most romantic gesture that we saw on *Sex and the City*. Even something as simple as a stranger giving up their subway seat has the potential to pull at a Miranda's heartstrings.

Unsurprisingly, Mirandas do not enter into new relationships casually. Every Miranda knows that love has the capacity to rob us of our dignity. We don't want to wake up one day and find ourselves beating the love of our life with our own wedding bouquet. Unfortunately, like your building going co-op, love can strike when you least expect it. One day, you're thriving, and the next, you're checking their Instagram stories on an hourly basis and and researching the best school districts for your hypothetical children. Whimsical thought patterns are a good indication that you may have found your better half, but that euphoric feeling can quickly give way to fear that your love may not be reciprocated. This compromised state can make a reasonably sane Miranda behave like a total Carrie, although we do stop short of stalking our partners' ex-wives. Our kind are more inclined to pick a fight with our partner for no apparent reason, then shut them out until we've had an adequate amount of time to process our feelings. This behavior lacks maturity and logic, but when a Miranda needs breathing room, she will go to any length to get it.

Commitment is terrifying, because it requires us to become utterly vulnerable—a weakened state that we spend our lives trying to avoid. It's easy for us to proclaim our undying love for things like TiVo, sex toys, or chocolate éclairs because unlike people, inanimate objects can never leave. But if you want to find the one, you must listen to your heart, not your head—even if both may be destroyed in the process.

Being successful in love begins with loving yourself. If we live in a state of inner turmoil, what hope do we have when a romantic partner is added to the equation? Contrary to popular belief, entering into a relationship will not fix what is already broken. We have to be self-sufficient, or at the very least self-aware, in order to have healthy relationships. We also have to take accountability for our own toxic behavior patterns. Throughout their romance, Miranda's judgmental nature pushed Steve to his breaking point.

Instead of empowering her partner, she attempted to browbeat him until he became the refined, ambitious person that she wanted. Of course, it didn't work, and she ultimately came to her senses. But this conflict serves as a reminder that you can't project a fantasy onto a person and then become angry when they don't live up to your expectations. People can only be who they are, not who you think they should be.

While Mirandas outwardly mock love and all its saccharine displays, deep down there is a romance novel–loving, basic bitch who wants to believe that the perfect person is out there. Our wariness about romance isn't born out of pessimism; it's a form of self-protection. When we run from relationships—or openly mock them—we are shielding ourselves from the sting of potential failure. Try as we might, though, we can't always resist the lure of love. It doesn't play by any rules—and certainly not our narrowly defined ones. We can fantasize about our perfect partner all we want, but love rarely takes the form that we think it will. If you are a Miranda who is looking for love, it is vitally important that you remain open to new people and experiences. You may have to go on some truly horrifying Bumble dates, but the Universe tends to favor the persistent.

Do not give up, or enter into a relationship of convenience (we're looking at you, Stanford and Anthony). A Miranda has to stay in the game, even when your efforts feel futile. In all likelihood, your Steve is out there somewhere on an equally bad date, wondering where the fuck you are.

Are They the One?

OR THE ONE FOR RIGHT NOW?

Good sex is a Miranda's blind spot. When we finally find a lover who can meet our needs, we become willing to look past the red flags that would normally send us fleeing for the exits. After all, who cares about emotional unavailability or anger issues when you're having multiple orgasms? Occasionally sex is so extraordinary that our minds actually trick us into thinking that we're in love with the person. The sexually inexperienced are particularly vulnerable to these delusions, as evidenced by the overly enthusiastic virgin that Samantha fucked in season three. Unfortunately, even the most seasoned Mirandas are capable of gaslighting themselves into believing that a good fuck is relationship material. So if you're attempting to navigate this whirlwind of emotions and erotic impulses, let the following flow chart be your guide . . .

Is It Love or Lust?

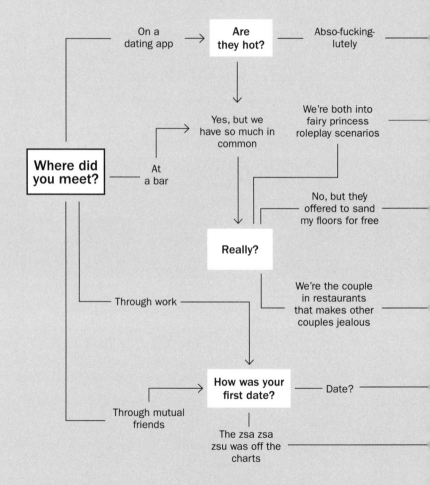

On a
dating app → **Are
they hot?** — Abso-fucking-
lutely

Yes, but we
have so much in
common

We're both into
fairy princess
roleplay scenarios

**Where did
you meet?** — At
a bar

No, but they
offered to sand
my floors for free

Really?

Through work — We're the couple
in restaurants
that makes other
couples jealous

**How was your
first date?** — Date?

Through mutual
friends

The zsa zsa
zsu was off the
charts

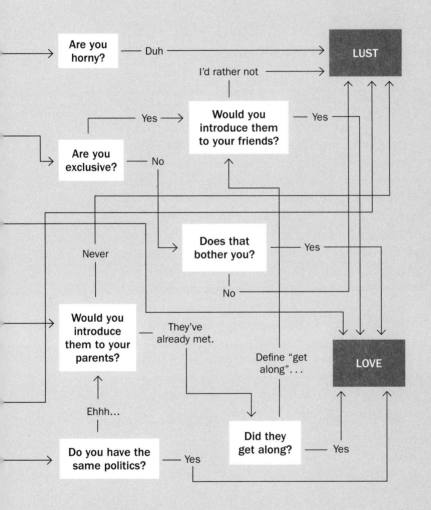

Humiliation Is Inevitable

Mirandas are homebodies by nature, so staying in and avoiding potentially triggering dating situations is a crucial form of self-preservation. After a string of humiliating romantic encounters, it's normal to want to barricade yourself inside your home with a pint of Häagen-Dazs and a *Forensic Files* marathon. However, there is a difference between self-care and avoidance. You may require solo time to recharge, but you can't shy away from the unpleasant aspects of dating. The truth of the matter is, finding someone you truly connect with takes time and a healthy dose of trial and error—which is usually where the indignity transpires.

Rejection is hard, and it inevitably takes a toll on your self-esteem. This can be particularly difficult for Mirandas, who are unusually prone to self-criticism. But without rejection, you cannot develop resilience. You also lose the opportunity to improve your dating skills. Some people are born with an innate gift for navigating the ins and outs of courtship. Others acquire dating acumen after years spent in the trenches.

The most important thing to remember is that rejection is universal. You're not the first person to hit on someone who wasn't interested in you. You certainly won't be the last person to be dumped. When you're coping with dating burnout, take a deep breath, regroup, and remind yourself that there is always some hot person somewhere who is totally down to fuck. You're unlikely to find them if you're too demoralized from dating a bunch of Skippers.

Which Asshole Are You Dating?

There are no good men, only assholes. Excuse the hyperbole, but let's face it—for every nice guy, there are fifteen sexual sociopaths who will fracture your psyche and compel you to return to the safety of your vibrator. But if the prospect of perpetual singledom is too much to bear, we're afraid the only way out is through . . . a bunch of assholes. Being with terrible men is not only necessary, but a prudent exercise in social anthropology and possibly the best sex of your life.

Assholes come in all shapes and sizes, with a wide range of personality defects, but there are a few key archetypes of male fragility and toxicity that will inevitably recur throughout your dating life. Once you've acquainted yourself with them, you'll be better equipped to flee before things get dark. Or you can keep dating them until they leave you at the altar. Your choice.

THE BERGER *THE TOXIC BETA BRO*

You've finally met your match. He's smart, funny, and fluent in banter. You're the couple other couples want to be. Enamored by his sensitivity and wit, you almost overlook the initial warning signs. It could be a passive-aggressive comment about your outfit or an overzealous appreciation for Woody Allen. Whatever it is, there's *something* a little bit off about this self-proclaimed feminist. The Berger exudes a nonthreatening beta energy, but just below that lies a simmering cavern of toxic masculinity. In reality, he employs the same unfortunate posturing tendencies of an alpha male, but obscures it with knitwear and an extensive vinyl collection. The Berger is frequently a creative type, making him especially prone to moodiness and underemployment. Which, in turn, leads him to resent you for having your shit together. Trying to make it work with a toxic beta bro will only leave you with a shattered sense of self-worth, or worse, a break-up via a Post-it Note.

THE AIDAN *THE JUDGMENTAL NICE GUY*

A hypermasculine straight guy with a sensitive soul is an anomaly, so we understand your attraction to The Aidan. This man will sand your floors for free and draw you a bubble bath when he senses that you *might* be stressed, but don't let the altruistic deeds and casual leather pants–wearing distract you from his subtle disapproval of your lifestyle. He may be overly judgmental about your vices, or try to pressure you into marriage when you are far from ready for it. Guys like this have a definitive vision of their future and will try to find a way to manipulate you into sharing that vision. The Aidan also has a tendency to hold grudges. He may claim to forgive and forget, but the microaggressions and gaslighting say otherwise. Conflict resolution is especially difficult with this type of man, because he is incapable of validating anyone else's point of view. While dating The Aidan has his perks—especially in the home improvement department—it can also lead to full-blown panic attacks at Kleinfeld's. Be true to yourself, or be doomed to conform to his basic narrative.

THE RICHARD *THE SOCIOPATHIC PLAYBOY*

If you're dating a Richard, you already know that he's an asshole. You don't begin a relationship with this type of man without an acute understanding of his workaholic and sociopathic tendencies. It's what imbues him with the confidence and capital that attracted you to him in the first place. He is an excellent lover, which is ultimately what trapped you into this soul-sucking psychosexual arrangement, but the real danger comes once you start to develop feelings for this man. When you fall for The Richard, you're fucked—and not in the way that you like. The highs are extremely high, but the lows will compel you to cry, scream, and destroy his possessions. This man is a serial cheater by nature and he will never change, despite his claims to the contrary. His overblown ego is fueled by power, money, and blowjobs from twenty-year-olds. So don't delude yourself into thinking that what you two have is special. Steer clear of The Richard at all costs—after all, a private jet is a poor substitute for a heart.

THE SKIPPER *THE NICE BETA BOY*

Okay, so The Skipper isn't exactly an asshole, but he isn't a keeper either. Sure, you will never have to suffer through a performative display of masculinity with this man, but you will have to deal with exceedingly boring dinners, lackluster sexual encounters, and post-date texting that borders on stalking. Dating The Skipper is tempting, because this guy is genuinely sweet, gainfully employed, and aims to make you feel cared for and respected. In today's treacherous dating landscape, ghosting someone who bought you flowers seems counterintuitive to say the least, but no amount of kindness can compensate for the fact that you two *do not have chemistry*. He may think otherwise, but you know that the magic simply isn't there. The Skippers of the world are like a flotation device, buoying you from your last shitty relationship into a less shitty one. So let him down easy—this asshole actually deserves it.

THE BIG *THE EMOTIONALLY UNAVAILABLE BIZ BRO*

This asshole is not for the faint of heart. He is charming and sophisticated, and his lack of emotional availability will slowly suck the life out of you. Keeping it casual isn't an option; you will always fall hard for this man. The balance of power is distinctly in his favor, yet you are oddly intoxicated by this regressive dynamic. The more withholding he is, the deeper you will dig in for any semblance of heartfelt intimacy. It's a vicious cycle of emotional highs and lows that you willfully suffer through because your inner Charlotte is convinced that things will work out. Your unwavering sense of optimism is delusional in this case, though, because The Big has given you many, *many* signals that he is not ready to let you in to his heart, or even his building. Even when you break things off, The Big has an uncanny ability to reappear at the exact moment that you are ready to move on. Like a bad Patrick McMullan party photo, this man will haunt you and your Google results until the day you die. Do yourself a favor and end this doomed romance before it even begins.

THE PETROVSKY *THE PRETENTIOUS ELDER*

He's older, he's worldly, and he's made some truly seminal large-scale light installations with integrated video imaging—but taking a *lover* who is a card-carrying member of the cultural elite often comes at a price. Your man is a genius, but his brilliance is fueled by long hours, unpredictable bouts of inspiration, and intermittent periods of depression. His creative output isn't just work—it's his fucking *identity.* Maintaining that identity will always take precedence over your relationship. The Petrovsky is smooth and impeccably cultured, and his lack of interest in adhering to arbitrary social norms is genuinely refreshing. He possesses a unique sense of self-awareness that many of your suitors lack, but his ways are set in stone. Surprises and spontaneity will not go over well with this man, so don't even *think* about booking an impromptu vacation or couples' massage. Despite his bohemian qualities, The Petrovsky is a control freak through and through. And while he may not be a bad person to date, he is definitely not marriage material. Come for the fabulous dinner parties and the romantic strolls through Central Park, but leave before you start talking about vasectomy reversal.

75

Men Are Like Cabs

"It's not fate, his light is on." So goes Miranda Hobbes's pragmatic takedown of Charlotte's newfound romance with Trey, a man she met two weeks prior and believes to be The One. Miranda's thesis is thus: men are like cabs, and when they are ready for a serious relationship—one that could culminate in marriage—their metaphorical light is turned on. Whoever enters the cab next (i.e., the next like-minded woman he meets) will swiftly become his bride. Miranda's theory challenges the notion that these bachelors have finally found their soulmates; instead, their sudden desire to get married is a survival instinct, motivated by the sudden realization that they do not want to die alone.

Emotional unavailability from men is almost a given in heterosexual dynamics. That is why women look for external signifiers to gauge a man's level of interest. Charlotte asserts that the Cartier watch that Trey bought her early in the relationship was a signal that she was the one. Conversely, Carrie knows that Mr. Big isn't on the same page as her when he is unwilling to give her so much as a drawer at his apartment. In retrospect, Mr. Big couldn't have given her more overt signals that his light was off. The swan-shaped clutch and the solo flight to Paris were equally good indicators.

Don't be fooled, though: women have the ability to be just as emotionally unavailable as men. Just look at Carrie and Aidan's shitshow of a relationship. The woman wore her engagement ring as a necklace, for God's sake! This passive-aggressive gesture practically screamed "I'm not ready to commit." So while Aidan's light may have been on, Carrie had no interest in getting in his car. That ride was a one-way trip to a cabin in Suffern.

So while Miranda's theory can help us lessen the sting when a relationship fails, we also have to hold ourselves accountable. Throughout the series, Miranda's light went on and off with abandon. Her relationship with Steve had its ups and downs, not because they weren't right for each other, but because of bad timing. When he wanted to settle down, she was focused on making partner. When she ultimately achieved that goal, the relationship failed. Then when she was ready to rekindle the romance, he was dating another woman. It took a leap of faith on Miranda's part and a declaration of devotion over a washing machine for their love story to finally sync up. So while her taxi analogy may seem most applicable to the niche of New York bachelors in their mid-thirties, its central thesis rings true for all: yes, ladies, timing is everything.

Ten Things to Do When
You've Been Dumped

Whether it happens in person, on a Post-it, or via a doorman, there is no good way to get dumped. Even the most level-headed Miranda can be blindsided when she finds herself on the receiving end of a breakup. Getting dumped crushes what little self-esteem you have and feeds that deeply cynical part of yourself that believes that the pursuit of love is bullshit. After all, who needs romance when you have alcohol and Amazon Prime? If you're in the thick of it, just remember that like last season's Saint Laurent, this too shall pass. For those of you who are desperately trying to get back on track, here are a few time-tested tips and tricks to help your ego recover.

1. Eat your feelings.

2. Call in sick.

3. Invest in a new sex toy.

4. Run a marathon . . .

5. . . . or just watch a *Jules &
   Mimi* marathon.

6. Get a Brazilian.

7. Text your fuck buddy.

8. Wear fake nipples.

9. Change your bed karma.

10. Smoke a joint.

Queering Miranda

Miranda Hobbes's heterosexuality was affirmed in the third episode of *Sex and the City,* when she was set up with a woman by a well-intentioned colleague. Even though she insisted that lesbianism wasn't for her, queer fans of the show have always felt that Miranda was one of their own. Perhaps it's her hair, or the fact that she famously berated the entire squad for their singular focus on men. Or maybe it's because within her social circle, Miranda was the least reliant on the opposite sex. Carrie needed men for her column, Samantha needed men for orgasms, and Charlotte was, well, Charlotte. Miranda ended up with Steve, of course, but she also lamented that he wasn't a "core-shaker" and seemed legitimately traumatized by their honeymoon. Between her repeated attempts to break up with Steve and her fondness for pantsuits, it's not hard to project a queer identity onto Miranda. Even though there were gay and bisexual characters on the series, Stanford, Anthony, and season four Samantha are far from complex and nuanced. Miranda may be straight, but she was the strong, gender-nonconforming icon that the LGBTQ community deserved.

If you're a queer Miranda yourself, congratulations! You'll have a far less complicated existence than the queer Charlottes. And as most of you already know, your sexuality and/or gender identity isn't immoral and tragic, it's an asset. Sure, the culture-at-large may oppress you and try to strip away your rights. But you know what? You have more class in your unusually long ring finger than they'll ever have.

Despite what basic Bible-thumpers claim, queerness has its benefits. Some of you can enjoy sex without the looming threat of procreation; others can share wardrobes with their partners. Queer Mirandas can also take pride in the litany of iconic cultural contributions from the LGBTQ community—including *Sex and the City*. Sure, Candace Bushnell wrote the book, but the series wouldn't have materialized without its two openly gay masterminds, Michael Patrick King and Darren Starr. Carrie would not be the fashion icon that she is without the trailblazing costume designer (and power lesbian) Patricia Field. And, of course, Miranda Hobbes as we know her could not exist without the regal, unapologetically out Cynthia Nixon. So if you ever feel alienated because of your otherness, just remember that Ms. Nixon is an Oscar away from completing her EGOT. Trust us, you're just as fabulous, too.

The Dos and Don'ts of Long-Distance Relationships

Here's a tip for surviving a long-distance relationship: *don't be in one*. Dating someone who lives in Queens is hard enough; dating someone who lives in another state or country is a fucking *nightmare*. Romantic relationships are typically defined by the presence of love and sex, whereas long-distance relationships are defined by sadness and involuntary celibacy. Living hundreds of miles away from the person who you rely on for companionship and orgasms completely defeats the point of having a relationship.

Should you happen to find yourself in the thick of a long-distance romance, it's probably because you had no other choice. Suitable dating partners can be shockingly scarce, especially when you enter your thirties and start to develop standards. If you're lucky enough to encounter a Harry Goldenblatt outside of your time zone, don't let them go. Just be prepared for lots of crying, failed Skype calls, and overly dramatic airport reunions.

DO PLAN AHEAD Long-distance relationships are far more bearable when you know when you are going to see each other again. Having a reunion date circled in your calendar will give you both peace of mind when things get rough. And things *will* get rough.

DON'T FREAK OUT WHEN EVERYTHING ISN'T PERFECT You've finally reunited, but it's not exactly the fairy-tale scenario that you envisioned. Don't worry—that's normal. Couples that have a limited amount of time to spend together often feel pressured to make every moment perfect, but life doesn't work that way. Don't feel bad if you have an off day.

DO TALK ABOUT CHEATING Is sexual fidelity actually realistic? It's up to both of you to decide. Monogamy and nonmonogamy are both flawed institutions, so we won't judge either way. A long-distance relationship puts a unique strain on couples, so have a civilized Samantha and Smith Jerrod–esque discussion about your options.

DON'T STAY IN ALL THE TIME Your lover may be confined to a screen for the foreseeable future, but that doesn't mean that you should spend all of your free time having marathon Skype sessions. Make sure that you prioritize your IRL relationships as well; it's important for your mental health *and* you'll get a much-needed break from your lackluster Wi-Fi connection.

DO HAVE FACETIME SEX It's certainly not *sex* sex, but FaceTime sex is better than nothing. And this should go without saying, but never attempt to juggle more than one long-distance sex partner at a time. This sex is a last resort, not a lifestyle. Don't be like that two-timing phone sex guy that Miranda fucked in season three.

DON'T STAY LONG-DISTANCE A permanent long-distance arrangement may have worked for Carrie's personal butler in *Sex and the City 2*, but we suspect that man's life was actually a living hell. One or both of you will have to relocate to make this relationship work in the long term. So if a move is off the table, end things now.

"

Soulmates only exist in the Hallmark aisle.

"

Codependency
Is for Charlottes

THE IMPORTANCE OF AUTONOMY

Every long-term relationship has a degree of codependency. Whether it's having a significant other pick up your dry cleaning or support you emotionally, we all rely on our partners to some extent. After all, one of the biggest perks of being part of a couple is having the ability to pool your resources to advance your shared goals. Utility bills become cheaper, your support system becomes wider, and you always have a shoulder to cry on—or cling to—in the event of an emergency. But while there are certainly many positives to pairing off, some people take this mutually beneficial dynamic *way* too far. That is the nature of codependency, and it's one of the most unfortunate qualities that a woman can acquire. Like pink carnations and men who wear square-toed shoes, codependency should be avoided *at all costs*. A truly codependent relationship will slowly rob you of your personality, your will to live and, ironically, with time, your relationship. So, if you have any interest in retaining your dignity, read on for the dos and don'ts of coupledom.

DO BE TRUE TO YOURSELF Committing to someone does not mean appropriating their interests, values, or behaviors as your own. You should certainly *know* a thing or two about the things that your partner cares about, but if you don't give a shit about football, don't pretend to give a shit about football. Never let yourself become one of those people who completely changes their personality to suit a new relationship, because those people are categorically the worst.

DON'T RELY SOLELY ON YOUR PARTNER FOR EMOTIONAL SUPPORT Or vice versa. Your partner should be the first person that you talk to if you are going through something difficult, but they should *never* single-handedly carry the burden of pulling you out of your funk. That's what friends, family members, and therapists are for.

DO MAINTAIN A HEALTHY DISTANCE You may live with your partner for years, even decades, but that doesn't mean that the two of you should be together 24/7. Never leaving your partner's side isn't a sign of your unwavering commitment; it's a sign that you no longer have the ability to function as an individual. Give your partner space, or risk becoming so codependent that you're both comfortable shitting with the door open—a true low.

DON'T ABANDON YOUR FRIENDSHIPS Being in a long-term relationship should *never* affect your friendships, and if it has, there is probably something wrong with your partner. Friends are crucial, because they provide you with a support system that is likely to outlast your current romance. And remember, it's equally important that your significant other has friends. You know who didn't have his own friends? Mr. Big. Enough said.

DO KNOW WHEN TO SAY "WE" There are legitimate reasons to say "we," such as "We are trying to have a baby," or "We are moving to Park Slope." However, the compulsive overuse of the term "we" is a bad look, not to mention potentially triggering for your single friends. Never say "we" if "I" is equally appropriate.

DON'T ENABLE EACH OTHERS' BAD HABITS If your partner looks past your workaholic tendencies, so you in turn overlook their alcoholic tendencies you are engaging in the worst kind of co-dependent behavior that there is. This ship is going *down,* and hitting rock bottom is not going to be pleasant for either of you. If you find yourself in a relationship like this, find a therapist and extricate yourself immediately.

DO LOOK AFTER YOUR FINANCES You may trust your partner implicitly, but if you share a bank account, you need to ensure that your financial stability is *not* contingent upon the success of the relationship. For centuries, women have stayed in bad relationships because they had no financial autonomy. Plan ahead so you never feel trapped should shit hit the fan.

DON'T ASSUME THAT YOU'LL ALWAYS BE TOGETHER This one is especially hard to hear. We all want to believe that our romances will last a lifetime, but in reality, couples get divorced and people *die*. If you spend your entire life in a codependent relationship, you will not be able to function outside of said relationship. You will lack the fundamental skills that are necessary to survive, and you will have no real identity of your own to fall back on. The key to long-term happiness is not being in a relationship, but being secure enough with yourself to live without one.

Skipper, It's Over

HOW TO BREAK UP WITH DIGNITY

Being dumped is soul-crushing, but being the person who does the dumping is its own kind of hell. First, you have to deal with the anxiety that comes with knowing you have to end a relationship. This becomes doubly hard when you still have feelings for your soon-to-be ex. It's a full-fledged fucking *nightmare* if they are completely in love with you. While you may be a heartless monster—in your own mind, anyway—there are several strategies that you can employ to make an impending breakup as humane as possible.

1. **RIP OFF THE BAND-AID** Breakups can go one of two ways. They can be fast and painful, leaving at least one partner completely blindsided, or they can be slow and painful, where you both

know that the relationship is doomed but you choose to pro-long it to avoid the initial shock of a breakup. Neither of these options is good, but one of them is worse. Get your shit together and end it.

2. **DON'T PULL A BERGER** Breaking up in person is uncomfortable, but it's the only way to exit a relationship with any integrity. Ending a romance over the phone, via a text message, or on a fucking Post-it is profoundly disrespectful. And don't even think about ghosting.

3. **BE FIRM** Do not so much as hint at a future reconciliation. It can be tempting to do so in the moment because you just want the person to feel better, but continuing to lead on an ex is profoundly cruel. Let them abandon all hope of being with you, so they can move on to someone who actually wants to be with them.

4. **DON'T CHECK IN** Establishing a friendship with an ex is healthy, but compulsively checking in on them in the immediate after-math of a breakup will simply prolong both of your suffering. If you're looking to alleviate your own guilt, do the right thing and leave them alone.

5. **AVOID DIGITAL DRAMA** Unless your ex-lover treated you like shit, there's no reason to swiftly erase their presence from your social feed. They may erase you—or even block you— but that doesn't mean that you need to be equally petty.

6. **DON'T FLAUNT YOUR REBOUND** Whether you left them for someone else or simply moved on quickly, it's poor form to broadcast your new relationship to the general public. Date whoever you want, but maintain a degree of privacy until the dust has settled.

Ex and the City

The relationships that we have with our exes speak volumes about our character, or in some instances, our self-destructive dating patterns. Some of us cultivate close friendships with people who we used to fuck, while others only initiate contact in the event of a chlamydia diagnosis, but in the age of social media, completely denying the existence of your ex is no longer an option. Even if we rarely encounter them in the wild, we still have to peacefully coexist online. Whether you're newly single or contemplating a reunion, here are some techniques to help you navigate the complicated landscape of post-breakup conduct.

How to Be Friends with an Ex

TO BE FRIENDS, OR NOT TO BE FRIENDS?
Being friends with an ex should not be the default setting for every failed romance. Relationships end for a myriad of reasons. Some of those reasons are bittersweet, like bad timing, while others are just bitter—like betrayal. If your union dissolved because of a major

violation of trust or mistreatment, a friendship is ill-advised. Your dynamic will be no less toxic as friends than it was when you were a couple. But if the relationship ended with both parties' dignity relatively intact, a mutually supportive, platonic relationship could be in the cards.

TAKE A BREATHER

Like training a puppy, cultivating a friendship with an ex takes time and patience. It won't happen overnight. There are too many raw feelings to process and too much blame to assign. A cooling-off period that lasts months—if not years—is advisable in many instances. Some exes cannot attempt a friendship until both parties have moved on to other partners. Don't fret if one or both of you isn't ready to transition into the next phase of your relationship. Just because you can't sustain a friendship now doesn't mean that you won't be able to in the future.

FRIENDSHIP IS NOT FOREPLAY

Many exes cultivate friendships that serve as a stopgap between being single and getting back together. This may have worked for Miranda and Steve, but most estranged couples are not made to last. The vicious cycle of breaking up and getting back together will only retraumatize both of you. If your so-called friendship is really just an excuse to transition back into dating, figure out what you actually want and act accordingly.

MY BOUNDARIES, MYSELF

When making the transition from romance to friendship, establishing boundaries is essential. An impromptu deep dive into their sex life—and yours—should be off-limits. Carrie learned this the hard way when Mr. Big described fucking his stiletto-clad movie star girlfriend over steak and martinis. The mental images of an ex's intimate life can be triggering and near impossible to erase. The goal of a post-breakup friendship is to eradicate sexual tension and jealousy, not heighten it, so even if you two have a history of sharing every detail of your lives, certain things are better left unsaid.

EMBRACE YOUR INNER POWER LESBIAN

Committing to someone till death do us part is a *very* tall order. Just because two people are incapable of making things work *forever* shouldn't mean that they can't have a relationship at all. That said, close friendships among heterosexual exes are exceedingly rare, unless a child or a business is involved. They also aren't totally socially acceptable, if early-aughts R&B songs are any indication. This is one (of many) areas where straight people can take a cue from lesbian culture. Queer women are notorious for cultivating deep, decades-spanning friendships with their exes. There are exceptions, of course, but for the most part, friendships between former couples in the queer community are celebrated, not scrutinized.

How to Avoid an Ex
Spoiler Alert: You Can't

LOCATION, LOCATION, LOCATION

Unless they move to Napa or suddenly drop dead, running into an ex is inevitable. Even if you don't physically cross paths with them, the mere sight of their favorite coffee shop or a single playing card lying on the street could be enough to trigger a meltdown. If you're in the throes of a painful breakup, the first order of business is to minimize triggers. Avoid any and all places where you might see them, or even *think* of them. If that means taking a different route to work in the morning or shunning your go-to cocktail joint on the weekends, so be it.

MUTE THE PAIN
Some breakups necessitate unfollowing, blocking, or getting restraining orders. If your former partner is cruel or abusive, feel free to block them *and their entire social circle*. But if you're simply recovering from a broken heart, muting should be sufficient. It's less dramatic than unfollowing and you can reconnect with them later without the added embarrassment of a push notification.

DON'T BE A STALKER
This should go without saying, but do not stalk your ex or their new partner on social media. Sure, there is a zero percent chance that any living, breathing Miranda will actually heed this advice, but we need to clearly state that this is the most sound path to take if you have any interest in moving forward in life. Obsessing over their obnoxious couples' Boomerangs will only make you bitter.

HIDE BEHIND A TELEPHONE POLE
Most of us don't have the luxury of having the new Yankee on our arm when we run into our ex, so if you happen to spot your former flame in the wild and they haven't noticed you, by all means, hide behind a telephone pole. An unexpected run-in with an

acquaintance is grating enough, but a surprise encounter with an ex can ruin your entire week. Avoidance is not the most mature route to take, but self-preservation is more important than exchanging pleasantries.

DO NOT RE-ENGAGE

If you are caught off-guard by a relatively pleasant run-in with your ex, do not panic and accidentally make plans with them. We saw Carrie do this in season two, when she became frazzled and invited Mr. Big to her birthday party. Impromptu invites happen when you didn't expect to see your ex, but you want them to know that you've moved on. Reinitiating contact can only lead to awkwardness, sadness, or the worst-case scenario: rejection. Be polite, and leave it at that.

Maybe There Isn't Someone for Everyone

YES, WE SAID IT

If hell exists, it's probably an endless stream of stop-and-chats with married acquaintances who ask you if you're seeing anybody special—and you aren't. After all, having to talk about your relationship status with relative strangers is one of the most triggering aspects of being single, especially when you are quickly reassured that the right person is "still out there" and "you just haven't met them yet." But *are* they still out there? Miranda Hobbes had an encounter like this in season four, but instead of affirming her acquaintances' theory that her soulmate was still at large, she said what no woman is ever supposed say: "*Maybe there isn't someone for everyone.*" And you know what? She was right.

The concept of The One gives all of us hope. It makes us feel like all of our failed relationships and unfortunate sexual encounters will ultimately culminate in a Hallmark Channel-esque romance that will solve all of our problems. But in reality, none of us are guaranteed love. Some of us will have fairy-tale marriages, while others will be die alone and be eaten by their cats. Even more of us will settle for a romance that is less than perfect because we can't stand the prospect of being alone. This all may sound harsh, but the world *is* harsh. Contrary to popular opinion, ditching our overly romantic notions about the way it operates is an act of agency—not defeat.

That said, if you're single or in a dead-end relationship, don't throw in the towel. After all, having optimism is essential for one's spiritual and mental health. However, there is a difference between being optimistic, and harboring delusions about what the world supposedly owes you. You need to understand that The One is a possibility, not a certainty. It's a concept that sells romcoms and self-help books to Charlottes, rather than a fact of life. Yes, you *could* accidentally trip in front of a taxi and end up meeting your future spouse—but you could also be run over by said cab and never live to see your forties. None of us are *guaranteed* a great love that is worthy of a Nicholas Sparks novel, and the quicker you internalize that, the better.

While you can't always control the path that your life takes, you can always control the choices that you make in the present moment. If finding great love is your number one priority, you need to (gently) put this book down and find the closest singles bar. Consistently putting yourself out there—despite the humiliations—is the best way to ward off a lifetime of solitude. You also have to take charge of your own well-being and resist the urge to self-sabotage. The One may or may not materialize, but you will always be there to pick yourself up after every bad date and celebrate after every triumph. So be good to yourself, and know that your happiness is not contingent on a Mr. Big, or a Steve, or a Maria Diega Reyes. At the end of the day, you've got this. But overfeeding your cat isn't the worst idea, either.

How to Be a Bride
Without the Bullshit

THE MIRANDA'S GUIDE TO WEDDINGS

Mirandas are united by their aversion to sentimentality, particularly when it manifests itself in the form of an event where we are required to make small talk with acquaintances. Naturally, weddings are something we tend to avoid. Weddings involve a myriad of things that Mirandas would typically shun: posed photos, frilly floral arrangements, and copious yards of duchesse satin. Even if you have no matrimonial aspirations, you will be obligated to attend a wedding at some point in your lifetime. (And if there is a Charlotte in your friend group, you may have to go to several.) Like death, taxes, and Barneys warehouse sales, weddings are an inevitable part of life. Here is how to participate in this gratuitous ritual of performative love *without* losing your shit.

. . . as a Wedding Guest

Uh oh, you've been invited to a wedding that you are obligated to attend! Whether it's a long-lost college friend or a current colleague, you know that the emotional fallout from your absence would be more annoying than just going to the damn thing. The

good news is that being a wedding guest requires the least amount of commitment. You typically just have to make it through the ceremony and reception, although some brides are extra and will also subject you to a bridal shower, a bachelorette party, a night-before party, and a post-nuptial brunch. In some instances, the wedding you are attending might be of the dreaded destination kind. For Mirandas, this is a complete nightmare as it disrupts your carefully cultivated schedule and take-out routine. But what can you do? It's the happiest day of your acquaintance's life. There's nothing to do except buy the cheapest thing on the registry, pray that there's an open bar, and hope you're not stuck with guestbook duty.

. . . as a Bridesmaid

Fuck! Your close friend just asked you to be in her wedding party. You're trapped. Of course you *can't* say no; you simply must resign yourself to your fate. For the next six to twelve months you will be sitting bitch to the whims of the bride formerly known as your friend. Sure, being a bridesmaid *sounds* fun, but in reality, it's a sadistic ritual meant to test your friendships and personal taste. It requires you to act as a therapist, event planner, *and* personal assistant. Moreover, it's extremely time-consuming. Mirandas value their free time immensely, and sadly, your upcoming weekends will be consumed by wedding dress shopping, party planning, and a host of other prewedding activities.

Is there any upside to being a bridesmaid? That's debatable. The process is undoubtedly taxing on your mental health, your bank account, and possibly your intimate relationships. Then again, there is always the chance that you could fuck someone hot after the wedding. People rarely acknowledge it, but wedding receptions are basically mating grounds for single people who have had a few too many glasses of prosecco. Never discount the value of a one-night stand with someone at the wedding—just so long as it's not the groom.

. . . as a Bride

Oh shit, you're getting married! Now every sardonic thing you've ever said about weddings and their antiquated formalities will come back to haunt you. While you've reconciled your concerns about the act of marriage, the prospect of taking a starring role in an actual ceremony still leaves you feeling queasy. How can you participate in an institution that you've spent so many years mocking? Easy. Just because you've been to horrible weddings it doesn't mean that yours has to be horrible too. Most traditions can be modified or scrapped entirely—after all, many of these rituals stem from religions that you don't practice or Pinterest boards that you don't follow.

But a good rule of thumb for a minimally annoying wedding is: short ceremony, open bar, decent food, and good music. And remember, you don't have to spend a ton of money, either. Miranda and Steve had a very low-fuss, budget-friendly affair thankfully, sparing us from plotlines about them picking out wedding china.

Ironically, being a bride utilizes many of your core skill-sets as a Miranda: the planning, the critical reasoning, the countless Google Docs. But best of all, as the bride you get to spend a disproportionate amount of money on a single outfit without anyone judging you. So relax, don't feel pressured to wear white, and remember you're not just marrying your true love—you're legally bound to their family, too!

Love May Kill You

BUT THAT'S OKAY

Love is shitty because it is essentially an extreme form of submission. Once you fall for someone, your heart and sanity are suddenly in the hands of another person who may or may not have your best interests in mind. You can do everything right and plan for the future, but there's no guarantee that you'll get the relationship that you want or need. It's a truly horrifying reality, and so it comes as no surprise that romance sends many Mirandas running for the hills.

By definition, being open to love means making yourself vulnerable to heartbreak, and accepting that tragic possibility is doubly hard for a Miranda. We pride ourselves on our ability to accurately assess complicated situations so that we can avoid unpleasant outcomes. Unfortunately, love does not adhere to the pragmatism that we Mirandas hold so dear. Love is indefinable and unpredictable; it can make the even-tempered among us act like a Charlotte.

But while dropping your guard makes you susceptible to a range of unfortunate emotions, keeping those walls up poses an even bigger threat to your long-term happiness.

If you're lucky enough to have experienced romantic love, then you know that nothing else compares. It is better than any promotion or Hermès handbag. In fact, it's better than the entirety of Samantha Jones's season six wardrobe, and because it's so fabulous, one occasionally has to make bold and potentially humiliating gestures in the name of love. For example, you may have to reconcile with your estranged husband in the middle of the Brooklyn Bridge. You certainly run the risk of being stood up and wanting to jump off said bridge, but if you don't show up at all, the loss could be even greater. Being a bystander to love may save you from heartache, but it also robs you of knowing if you are loved in return.

Loving someone is a courageous act. It carries steep odds, with the transcendent feeling of true intimacy on one end, and a shame-spiral of emotional despair on the other. It's up to you to decide whether you want to show up for love, with all of its faults and complexities. It may break your heart, shatter your psyche, and leave you running around Manhattan in a beret with a McDonald's bag in hand, but what's the point of living if you're just going to play it safe? Even if things don't go your way, just remember that your friends are your soulmates anyway.

WHAT YOU SHOULD HAVE LEARNED FROM THIS CHAPTER

- Timing is everything.
- You will date a lot of assholes.
- Not all Mirandas are straight.
- You can never escape your ex.
- Codependency is unbecoming.
- Soulmates are for Carries.
- Sometimes he *is* that into you.
- Long-distance relationships are dramatic.
- Breaking up (with Skipper) is hard to do.
- Getting married is not in our nature—until it is.
- Humiliation is part of the dating process.

CHAPTER 4

WORK
LIKE
A
MIRANDA

You Better Work, Bitch

I Work, Therefore I Am

HOW TO SUCCEED IN BUSINESS
WITHOUT LOSING YOUR SHIT

Miranda Hobbes is an Ivy League–educated lawyer who made partner by the age of thirty-five. We'd venture to guess that most of you aren't quite as successful as she is, and that's perfectly fine.

Being a wealthy workaholic is not inherent to the Miranda personality type. Some of us are broke, and many of us aren't even terribly ambitious, but everyone has to make a living (well, everyone except the Charlottes of the world, who inherit multimillion-dollar apartments and docent as a hobby), but apart from those privileged few, work is not optional. Most of us have to devote the majority of our waking hours to our jobs. Some of us live to work, while others work to live. One approach is not better than the other, although we do applaud the work-to-livers for actually using their vacation days. No matter what camp you fall into, liking, or at the very least, tolerating the job that you have is a foundational element of a happy life. Hating what you do for a living will only make you bitter—and you've been bitter since grade school.

If you want to excel at your chosen profession, you must have tenacity. While Mirandas may enjoy a great deal of professional success throughout our lives, we are rarely what one would describe as an "overnight sensation." There are exceptions, of course, but for the most part, we have to put in a steady, prolonged effort to achieve our goals. Which means years—and potentially decades—of working hard, succeeding, fucking up, picking ourselves up, and repeating this vicious cycle no matter what. In an era of instant gratification, the prospect of spending years in the trenches is harrowing at best. Many of us can't handle waiting more than a few minutes for a latte, let alone years for a promotion or a degree. It is especially difficult when we see colleagues ascend, despite their own incompetence, through nepotism and cutting corners. The temptation to follow suit may be strong, but resisting will pay dividends in your future. Those who put in the long, hard hours will gain a savviness that cannot be acquired by those who fake it till they make it.

Just because we're Mirandas doesn't mean that we always have our shit together. Many of us are trapped in dead-end jobs, while others have enviable careers but sad, pathetic lives. If any of this sounds familiar, it's time to regroup. You only have one life. You don't want to spend it sitting in a cubicle, contemplating arson. The onus is on each Miranda to find a money-making endeavor that is fulfilling—or at the very least bearable. In the age of #girlbossing, it can feel like everyone and their mother is an entrepreneur. In reality, only a rare few will develop wildly popular apps and retire in their thirties. The more likely path for a Miranda is to either slowly ascend the corporate ladder in a career they enjoy *or* work a day job that supplements their true passion.

If you're unsure about the direction of your career, part-time jobs allow you to test out the various paths you may want to forge in life. And if you do know what you want, start plotting your next move now. We don't have unlimited time on this earth, as the late Lexi Featherston taught us.

Adaptability is also crucial for a Miranda's success. Those who cannot adjust to unforeseen changes in the workplace or learn from their own failures will never succeed. The most prolific Mirandas are able to own their mistakes—as well as their triumphs—and use them to propel forward. Our self-critical nature makes this easier said than done, but we must persevere. Only then can we develop alternate strategies that will prevent us from fucking up in the future.

Working like a Miranda isn't about having a corner office or a chic Jil Sander wardrobe. Instead, it's about knowing what you want in life and having the guts to go after it. It's also about resisting the temptation to throw in the towel when success eludes us. After a few too many hours on Instagram, it's easy to feel like you should be further along in your career—or your life, for that matter. But that feeling of inadequacy is a testament to the evils of social media, not your personal shortcomings. Coveting someone else's highly curated life robs you of energy that you should be channeling into your work.

At the end of the day, every Miranda must succeed on her own terms. For some, that means climbing to the top of the corporate ladder. For others, that means making large-scale vagina paintings in a barn in upstate New York. No matter your path, all Mirandas are imbued with a strong work ethic. We all have the capacity to be exceptional—we just need to find a niche that truly serves our talents. Our existential dread can only be exorcised by doing work that we are passionate about, not chasing success for the hell of it.

Whatever your dream is, pursue it. Always remember, though, that you are so much more than what you do for a living. Success can take on many forms, and not all of them involve six-figure salaries. Put in the hours, and see where things go. If you need to adjust your course along the way, so be it. You're in this for the long haul, and if you're anything like Miranda Hobbes, you'll kill it.

My Workspace, Myself

Lilacs from Steve

Portrait of Brady

He's Just Not That Into You

Bullshit Bagel

Palm Pilot

WE SHOULD ALL BE MIRANDAS

You can learn everything about a woman from her workspace. Some have clutter-free desktops and chic floral arrangements, while others hoard used Starbucks cups like they're going out of style. Most Mirandas fall somewhere in the middle. They know where their important documents are, but they probably have a desk drawer filled with old tabloids and discarded sugar packets. They enjoy the occasional bit of office decor, but reserve judgment for those who favor motivational quotes or shrine-like tributes to their kids. Achieving a functional balance between order and chaos is a constant struggle for a Miranda, and some are more naturally adept at taming clutter than others. Regardless of where you fall on the tidiness spectrum, your workspace is yours and yours alone. If a bit of clutter works for you, who cares what your Charlotte-identified colleagues think? Your workspace is sacred, so make it functional, make it personal, and never, *ever* let anyone borrow your stapler.

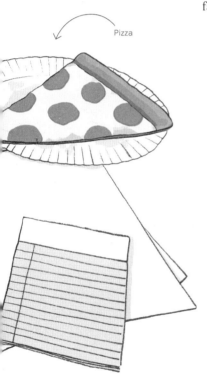

Pizza

Workaholics Get Shit Done

While we never saw Miranda Hobbes practice law in any capacity, her corporate attire and copious manila folders effectively communicated that she didn't fuck around when it came to work. Even though her closest friends had baller jobs as well, Miranda's intense workload and propensity for freaking the fuck out when she didn't have internet access quickly distinguished her from her peers. She was a workaholic, and this may or may not be a quality that you share with her.

For some, work can be a meditative practice. There is a certain peace that comes with tasks like clearing out your inbox or swiftly blowing through your to-do list. Many workaholics feel a deep sense of control when they are immersed in their jobs. This sense of well-being is further amplified by the addictive high of a professional triumph. Some may get their kicks from shopping or casually fellating the Worldwide Express guy, but given the choice between a late night at the office or a marginally satisfying sexual encounter, most Miranda-identified workaholics would pick the office. Really, who can blame them?

Workaholics get shit done, but it's not an easy path. Miranda Hobbes could not have bought her apartment or made partner at her law firm without years of diligent labor. Because of her workaholic tendencies, she had professional and economic advantages that provided her with a great deal of security. But while having the ability to buy Manolos is chill and all, it's a poor substitute for having an actual life. Workaholism should never be a lifelong strategy; it's best utilized for short-term goals like getting a promotion. If you do have workaholic tendencies, it's crucial that you assess the impact that it is having on you and those around you.

If your devotion to your career has negatively impacted your family or your relationships for a prolonged period of time, that is a serious problem. If your job has repeatedly affected your physical or mental health, that too is a major cause for concern. It's also important to consider *why* your job is so important to you. Do you love what you're doing? Or is economic security your primary concern? Do you actively enjoy spending endless hours at the office? Or are you using work to fill a void because other areas of your life are lacking? Being able to determine just how fucked up you are is crucial, because you don't want to end up sending Google Calendar invites from your deathbed. Work is important, but it isn't everything. And if your current life can be described in the phrase "work, work, Au Bon Pain, work," à la Miranda in season four, it might be time to rethink your priorities.

Make Google Docs Your Bitch

For better or worse, Miranda often chose her PalmPilot over basic human interactions. Her honeymoon was completely derailed by faulty cell phone reception and her TiVo often took precedence over dating and sex. Consistently an early adopter of new technologies, Miranda would be right at home in today's cloud-based, app-centric work world. But as new innovations simultaneously streamline and complicate our lives, remaining focused can be a challenge. If digital clutter and procrastination is turning you into a total Carrie, here's how to work smarter, not harder.

GOOGLE DOCS Do you like working with others, by yourself? Google Docs allows you to create and collaborate on everything from documents to spreadsheets and slide presentations remotely. You can easily monitor edits made by others and leave comments in-app. Be the office hero by exporting your work into a variety of formats to send to clients or share them via an emailed link.

BATTERY CASE A drained battery is a *nightmare* for a Miranda. You live your life on your phone, so invest in a battery case. Yes, they're about as aesthetically pleasing as Aidan's season three wardrobe, but a device that wirelessly charges your phone is much easier than hunting for a spare outlet at your local coffee shop.

WEBSITE BLOCKERS Sometimes the lure of celebrity gossip is too hard to resist for a Miranda—especially during the workday. A quick detour to *Oh No They Didn't!* or the *Daily Mail* are healthy, if empty, distractions to reset the brain, but if you can't keep this impulse in check, you might want to download apps that prohibit you from visiting these tempting sites. It's the digital equivalent of putting soap on a chocolate cake to keep yourself from eating it out of the garbage.

CLOUD BACKUP If backing up to an external hard drive is something that you can't commit to, then cloud services are for you. Our computers hold the digital net worth of our professional and personal lives. Losing that data to theft, malfunction, or ransomware is catastrophic, as Carrie learned in season four. For a small monthly fee, your information can be backed up to a cloud service that allows you to retrieve it anytime, anywhere.

EMAIL FOLDERS This one may seem antiquated, but if you have 5,456 unread emails in your inbox, take heed. Our inboxes have become digital dumpsters, where important work emails commingle with spam that we can't be bothered to unsubscribe from. Beginning to sort emails into folders by categories will lessen your inbox anxiety and make finding old emails a breeze. You can label them however you want: Work, Spam, Brady Hobbes-Brady.

Fuck You All

If you can't choose your family, and friends are the family that you choose, then coworkers are the friends you didn't choose and the family that you don't want. Sure, some Mirandas adore their colleagues and can't wait to go to work each day. If this sounds like you, you're probably a Miranda with a Charlotte rising and you can skip this section. But for everyone else, mind-numbing small talk and microaggressions from colleagues can be one of the more taxing aspects of our jobs. Oftentimes, we must maintain a facade at work, as our true selves are too bitchy to peacefully coexist with these people. It's exhausting, and it's definitely shaving years off of our lives, but while you can't always escape the people who you work with, you can employ strategies to make office life slightly more bearable.

Make One Work Friend

No one can be their own private island in an office environment. If this is what you truly desire, then freelancing may be more your speed. As such, it's worth making at least one work friend. The easiest way to do this is to find something to bond over with someone.

Maybe it's your shared love of *Jules & Mimi* or your mutual hatred for your boss. Having someone to talk shit with is crucial for your mental health, especially if you're in a relationship. Your partner shouldn't have to listen to you bitch about Denise from Accounting every single day.

Keep a Flask in Your Desk

We're not saying that you should make a habit of drinking on the job, we're just saying that *occasionally* a situation does call for it. Maybe you're going through a painful breakup, or facing a professional catastrophe that completely consumes you, or perhaps the long hours that you put in at the office prevent you from drinking at a bar like a normal person. Whatever it is, it can be good to have a flask on hand for emergencies. Just make sure to conceal it, because everyone has a meddling colleague who will not hesitate to fuck up your life.

Find Where the Line Is

A much healthier coping mechanism for all your office-related aggression is humor. That said, one person's joke is another person's insult, so before you start dishing out zingers, you need to determine if anyone around you will take offense. Knowing the comedic temperature of an office is crucial, because offending your colleagues will make your job even more unbearable. You may feel annoyed by your coworkers' mere existence, but you don't want to alienate them with an ill-timed joke. Doing so will cement your position as the asshole of the office. Remember, you're only one casual Friday away from accidentally outing a colleague.

Get Everyone Coffee

Just because you can't stand the people you work with doesn't mean you shouldn't do nice things for them. You cannot do your job in complete isolation, so you need to make the occasional gesture to ensure that relations will remain smooth. The best part is, offering to get everyone coffee will endear you to your coworkers *and* give you at least 20 minutes away from the office. Everyone knows how long those lines can be, so it's completely within reason to spend a little extra time running a personal errand or poring over the latest issue of *Tattle Tale.* As long as you come back with Becky's Frappuccino, no one will be the wiser. Work can consume our lives, so it's important to take time for yourself—even if it's under a false altruistic premise.

AND HERE'S A BONUS THING YOU SHOULD NEVER DO . . .

Do Not Fuck a Coworker

We get it, it's hard to meet people, especially when you're trapped in a cubicle for the majority of your waking hours. But however convenient, fucking a coworker is *never* a good look. It's hard enough to keep your personal life from bleeding into your work life—you don't need it to physically occupy the same space. If your boss or colleagues find out, they *will* judge you, and who can blame them? Office romances and their inevitable drama compromise the entire operation, so always remember to keep your inappropriate sexual impulses at bay, or at the very least, save them for that stranger in a sandwich costume.

The Miranda's Guide to Freelancing

After years of slogging through the corporate world, you finally get to call the shots. Congrats! Bask in the glory of self-employment while it lasts, because that warm feeling will quickly be replaced by the cold realization that *you are your own boss*. You may have the freedom to visit a museum on a Tuesday afternoon, but you will not have paid sick days, health insurance, or colleagues to rescue you in the event of a crisis. This lifestyle requires rigorous self-management, because the temptation to slack off is everywhere. Unlike in your corporate job, you don't get paid to watch cat videos when no one's looking.

Freelancing has its perks—flexible hours, minimal oversight, being able to masturbate in the middle of the day—but it is not for everyone. Some people feel isolated, while others find the lack of external motivation to be crippling, not liberating. A Miranda's ability to effectively manage her time will make or break her career.

Whether you're thinking about taking the plunge or are already working eighty-hour weeks from the comfort of your own bed, here are our essential tips for thriving as a solo agent.

Understand *How* You Work

Do you work best under pressure? In the morning? In solitude? This information is essential to your success as a freelancer. Defining and implementing practices based on your past successes (and failures) will maximize your output and ward off unnecessary chaos.

Getting Paid Is a Part-Time Job

Every freelancer will tell you that getting paid for your work is a job in and of itself. You may invoice immediately, but that doesn't mean that you'll be paid for days, weeks, or in many instances, months. The best course of action is to assume the worst, and set aside money in the event that multiple clients fuck you over.

Location, Location, Location

Your job may be a solitary affair, but that doesn't mean that you have to work in isolation. Some Mirandas are happy to work from home, while others require the hustle and bustle of a coworking space or coffee shop. Figuring out what works best for you will make you more productive *and* decrease your chances of turning into a cavewoman.

Meet Your Deadlines

This one is obvious. When an employer hires a freelancer, it means that they trust the person to do their job without being managed on a daily basis. Don't give your client a reason to feel like they need to manage you. As long as you get your work done on time, no one ever has to know that you lost half the day to a hangover.

Stick to a Schedule

Setting your own schedule is the number one benefit of working for yourself. It almost makes up for the fact that you have no other benefits, like financial security or clearly defined vacation days. If you're a night owl, you have the freedom to establish a semi-nocturnal workday. However, it's important to keep in mind that your clients—who do work normal hours—will still expect you to be available to them during their nine-to-five workday.

Put It in Writing

Many freelancers work without a contract—but it's not worth the risk. Having clearly defined deliverables can save you from a ton of extra work if your client is indecisive. It also protects you financially in the event that your client decides to ghost you. This happens way more often than it should, so it's best to be prepared.

Get Dressed

Working in your pajamas may seem like a dream, but after a couple of days, it becomes highly detrimental to your mental health. Just because you don't have to see other people doesn't mean that you should abandon one of the cornerstones of self-care. A Miranda should always *look* like she has her shit together, even if no one is around to see it.

"

I want to enjoy my success, not apologize for it.

"

Think Before You Reply All: The Miranda's Guide to Email

Gone are the days when email was reserved for frivolous pursuits, like eBay shopping or harassing your long-suffering ex with love letters from great men. Today, email is about effectively managing work-related communication in a timely fashion, often to the detriment of your personal life. Almost every job involves fielding a seemingly endless string of notifications from Gmail, and because we use email so frequently, blunders and faux pas aren't just likely, they're inevitable. Here are our go-to strategies for conquering the fraught landscape of digital correspondence.

Learn to Read Between the Lines

Work emails are all about subtext. There is a lot that your boss, colleagues, or clients are saying *without* saying it. For example, receiving a message from your boss that includes the phrase "just checking in" may sound chill, but it could indicate that your work is not up to snuff. That and phrases like "checking on the status of" or "circling back" are really just coded screams in lowercase for "*Where the fuck is that thing and why didn't I have it yesterday?!*" Likewise, a long overdue email reply that begins with "sorry for the delayed response" has less to do with a person's busy calendar and more to do with your low ranking on their priority list. The impulse to ghost them back may be strong, but it's important to email others how you would like to be emailed and not how they email you.

Drama-Free Attachments

Paper clutter is becoming obsolete, but email attachments are more popular than ever. If you don't know how to properly save or convert your files, it is of *paramount* importance that you learn right now. If we had a dollar for every time that we've received a .zip file that wouldn't open or an expired link to a Dropbox folder, we too would have $40,000 worth of shoes.

Do Not Log in to Your Personal Email at Work

This is absolutely crucial. Whatever you do on your work computer is technically your bosses' business. You definitely don't want to be fired for an email that you could have just sent from your phone. Additionally, it's appropriate to maintain a healthy dose of paranoia when it comes to your Gchat transcripts. Switching to "off the record" is a necessary form of protection when you are talking shit about anything pertaining to your job via your work email. Also, this should go without saying, but never, *ever* sync your iMessages to your work computer. When your boss comes over to check on that sales report, he or she is likely to see an incoming text from the Samantha of your group about funky-tasting spunk or something equally sordid.

The Dos and Don'ts of Email

- **DO NOT "REPLY ALL" TO A BCC WITH INFORMATION ONLY RELEVANT TO THE SENDER** We know the buttons are really close together, but nothing turns the whole office against you more than clogging their inboxes with a thread they can't get off of and never needed to be on in the first place.

- **DO "REPLY ALL" TO AN EMAIL YOU WERE CC'D ON** Reciprocally, don't be the person who shuts their coworkers out on pertinent information because you only replied to the sender.

- **DO NOT BLAST YOUR COWORKERS WITH BACK-TO-BACK ONE-SENTENCE EMAILS** Would you like your inbox blown up by multiple emails sent minutes apart? No, because you're not a psychopath. Draft a single, concise paragraph instead.

- **DO NOT SEND WORK EMAILS PAST MIDNIGHT** We're sure that idea you had at 2:00 a.m. is life-changing, but it can wait. Sending work emails way past office hours is borderline abusive and will breed resentment from your colleagues.

- **DO WRITE THAT EMAIL AND SAVE IT YOUR DRAFTS, THOUGH** Sending emails during work hours demonstrates that you respect your coworkers' boundaries and their right to personal lives. Sitting on an email will also save you from making the previously mentioned email blunders.

- **DO KEEP IT IN ONE THREAD** Consolidating your correspondence into a single, searchable email thread is the only way to live. Multiple threads about the same topic encourage disorganization and test your sanity when you actually need to find something.

EMAIL GREETING DECODER

Dear	Your mom is emailing you
Hi All,	A person asserting that there are too many people on this email
Hello,	A person who doesn't know your name and will never learn it
To Whom This May Concern,	A potential intern or a college loan officer who figured out your work email
No greeting, just your name	Your boss letting you know he's a cool boss, but he/she still owns you

EMAIL SIGNATURE DECODER

Cheers,	A basic person trying to be cool
Best,	A person who fucking hates you and can barely hide their contempt
xx	A coworker who def wants to fuck you
All My Best,	A coworker who might want to fuck you
Best Regards,	A person who doesn't expect or want a reply
[no signature]	A person trying to assert their dominance over you

Everybody Cries
in the Bathroom

Look—work is stressful. Whether you have a career that you love or a survival job for the paycheck, shit can get overwhelming. Mirandas have high standards in general, but the standards that we set for ourselves and our performance at work are borderline psychotic.

We like being in control, and we feel a deep sense of discomfort when that sense of control starts to slip away. Perhaps your boss treats you like garbage. Maybe your clients are satanic, or you hit "Reply All" at the worst possible time. Any number of things can leave you feeling overwhelmed and momentarily render you useless at work. Most of the time you can calm yourself with a well-timed Starbucks run or a therapeutic Gchat session with a like-minded colleague. Other times, there is no way off the panic train. Crying is inevitable, and you're fucked.

While one should avoid crying *in front* of people at work, that doesn't mean that you shouldn't cry *at* work. It's all about location. If you're lucky enough to have your own office, à la Ms. Hobbes, your adventure stops here. Tell your assistant to hold your calls, close the door, and let the tears flow. For those of you who work in a cubicle or an open office, the bathroom is your refuge. It's not ideal, and if you stay in there too long your colleagues will think that you're taking a shit—which is arguably worse—but you're fresh out of options. You will have to cry in a relatively efficient manner so that no one can link you to your emoting. It's a smart idea to wear sunglasses when you enter the bathroom and keep them on when you leave. Ideally, you should also try to MacGyver some sort of cold compress out of paper towels and ice cubes to reduce the swelling in your face.

If you're reading this and thinking that it's fucked up to develop a strategy to conceal your pain, you're not wrong. There should be less stigma around crying in public. Until that oppressive cloak of shame is lifted, though, you sure as hell aren't going to be a pioneer.

People Are Funny About Money

ASKING FOR A RAISE, THE MIRANDA WAY

The single joy of a nine-to-five life is a consistent paycheck. That said, if you're not being paid what you're worth, resentment is inevitable. You'll have to ask for a raise, but that comes with its own complications. Talking about money is almost always uncomfortable, especially when you have to broach the topic with a boss or higher-up who you aren't exactly close to. Awkwardness aside, being able to assert your worth to an employer is one of the most important skills that a Miranda can acquire. Like sex, you'll only get good with practice and a decent amount of confidence. Whether you're a virgin or a seasoned pro, here are five essential strategies to help you negotiate your salary like a Miranda.

DO YOU DESERVE A RAISE? Look, we all *want* more money. After all, being financially stable is the ultimate status symbol for the Miranda-identified. However, your work may not warrant a raise. We don't mean to be harsh, but the simple act of showing up for work every morning and not murdering all of your colleagues doesn't make you Sheryl Sandberg. Unless you are being paid less than the industry standard or become aware of a major wage disparity in your workplace, don't ask for a raise if your work isn't up to snuff. Those who are chronically undervalued—and can prove it—may ask for a raise at any time. But if your output leaves something to be desired, don't expect a raise just because you've put in the hours.

BUILD A CASE You don't have to have a law degree to prove beyond a reasonable doubt that you deserve a raise, but it's important to remember two truths about salary negotiations. Firstly, you're not a selfish person to ask for a raise, and secondly, your company isn't going to part with more money than they need to. Remember not to rely on emotion, but to simply state the facts. Showcase the value that you've added to the projects you've overseen, and if that doesn't work, try quantifying how much they would lose if you left. You shouldn't threaten them outright, but some subtle negging may be in order. Lastly, while you want to be thorough, you also need to be concise. Make your point and make it brief, because your bosses don't want to talk about money, either.

KNOW WHEN TO ASK As a Miranda, you already have the good sense to not ask for a raise if you've been at the company for less than a year. Likewise, if your company isn't doing well, it's not the time to ask for a salary increase. Timing is everything. The best way to ensure you get that financial glow-up is to build off the momentum of your stellar work. Try scheduling a salary discussion or a performance review close to when a big project—one you were vital to—has finished. Employers' memories are notoriously short, so make sure to maximize the benefits of your professional triumphs.

ACT THE PART Talking about money is uncomfortable enough, but asking someone in a position of power to *give* you money can be positively unnerving. If you don't possess the self-confidence that is necessary to effectively ask for a raise, you must pretend like you do. Yes, ladies, faking it is not limited to the bedroom! While you should be judged on the merit of your work alone, employers respond to confidence. Make sure to hold eye contact, and if you feel yourself starting to slip, just imagine that you're Samantha in her most fabulous neon power suit and assertiveness will follow.

AND IF YOU DON'T GET A RAISE . . . Well, shit. That didn't go as planned. If you don't get that raise on the first try, be gracious. Asking for a salary increase does not automatically mean that you'll get one. If the answer is no, ask your employer for feedback as to why the timing isn't right. Give yourself goals and assign a date in the future to readdress this topic. If civility isn't in the cards, you can always quit, especially if you feel like your bosses are baiting you with a promotion or a raise that will never come. It's easy to delude yourself into believing that you'll never find a job as good as the one that you currently have, but as Miranda Hobbes learned in the second film, there are actually chill law offices that hold meetings outdoors where everyone eats giant salads. Sometimes the best way to achieve your professional nirvana is to take your talents elsewhere.

When to Leave a Job

HOW TO KNOW WHEN YOU'RE IN A TOXIC
RELATIONSHIP WITH YOUR EMPLOYER

Knowing when enough is enough isn't just a quandary for Carrie's column, it's an important metric for your shitty job as well. Financial security is precious, so quitting can feel counterintuitive, if not downright scary—but every Miranda has her limits. We witnessed Ms. Hobbes reach hers in the second film when her boss assigned her case to another, more *male* lawyer. Discrimination and harassment are always valid reasons to quit your job (and threaten legal action); however, most difficult work situations are rarely this clear-cut.

Let's say your company takes on a project or a client that violates your personal code of ethics. This might feel wrong to you, but it's not illegal. Sometimes, it's worth bending your moral compass a *tad* if it gives you the power to effect broader change within the institution later. But if you feel like you are compromising your morals on a regular basis, it's time to put in your two weeks' notice. Quitting often feels like a privilege that most of us don't have, but some situations *require* us to escape, regardless of the financial recourse. For instance, no job is worth sacrificing your happiness, despite what *The Devil Wears Prada* taught us. Your job should challenge you, not destroy you. Offices that cultivate an overly stressful work environment can and will wreak havoc on your mental health. Those who are predisposed to depression and anxiety should flee *immediately*. You may end up taking a significant pay cut, but not crying in the shower every morning is priceless.

Oftentimes, the most complicated work situations involve our bosses. There is a very fine line between constructive criticism and abuse. Some bosses push us because it's in the best interest of the company, whereas others are sadistic assholes who get off on asserting their dominance, a.k.a. The Richard Wrights of the world. It is imperative that you learn to distinguish between the two. It's also important to keep your relationship with your boss as clear-cut as possible. Running personal errands or becoming their de facto therapist in times of crisis can quickly lead to dark places. When the lines between an employer and an employee get hazy, dysfunction is inevitable. If your bosses' overreliance on you starts borders on codependency, navigate your exit strategy.

Because Mirandas are inherently stubborn and goal-oriented, their desire to persevere is strong. But sometimes this instinct can backfire. If you've stuck with a less-than-fabulous job for ages because you *think* that conditions will improve, you're probably wasting your time. Staying at a job for longer than you should is *never* advisable. Like dead-end relationships, we can cling to dreadful jobs for years to avoid change. Being Mirandas, our minds tend to run wild with the fear of the unknown. *What if I'm unemployed for months? What if I make less money? What if my next job is even worse than the one I left? What if I make a huge mistake by leaving?* At a certain point, you have to ask yourself: *What if my job is slowly killing me?* As Steve advised Miranda, "Life is too short. Go somewhere where they appreciate you."

WHAT YOU SHOULD HAVE LEARNED FROM THIS CHAPTER

- Workaholism has its benefits.
- Hating your colleagues is normal.
- Crying at work can be therapeutic.
- Freelancing is not for the faint of heart.
- Most emails are thinly veiled threats.
- Your desk is your sanctuary.
- Know what you're worth.
- Back up your fucking computer.
- Don't forget to "reply all."
- You are more than your job.

CHAPTER 5

FUCK LIKE A MIRANDA

Miranda Hobbes Knows Good Sex—
And Isn't Afraid to Ask for Oral

Getting the Fuck You Want

...OR AT THE VERY LEAST,
FINDING THE VIBRATOR YOU NEED

Who says that humiliating sex is reserved for your twenties? If you're not careful, it can occupy a good portion of your thirties, too. Being a Miranda means knowing what you want from a sexual partner, but probably not finding it on the first, second, or twentieth try. This mildly dehumanizing process of elimination can easily wreak havoc on our psyches and our bed linens. But we know that good sex is out there, and we are willing to sacrifice our dignity, self-worth, and the very will to live in pursuit of it. We'd like to think that this isn't the case, but when a Miranda is deprived of a sexual outlet, she slowly descends into madness. Whether she's flirting with a grown man in a sandwich costume or screaming "I need to get laid!" at a lecherous construction worker, standards are nowhere to be found in the event of a dry spell. The only way to completely avoid these embarrassing lapses of judgment is to enter into a long-term relationship. Mirandas who have a fulfilling sex life at home rarely feel the need to seek out randoms to fuck. But if that special someone happens to be as elusive as a pair of Manolo Blahnik mary janes, thankfully you have other options.

As many of you already know, good sex starts at home—with yourself. How will you ever figure out what you like if you aren't willing to put in the work? You can't expect a partner to do it for you. Taking the time to understand the unique mechanics of your body is absolutely imperative. When you know what gives you pleasure, you can then impart that information to others. Choosing to remain willfully ignorant will only result in a lifetime of sexual encounters that are far more mediocre than you realize. However, the real joy of solo sex is having the opportunity to connect with yourself. You can lay back, relax, and let your mind (or your preferred porn genre) do the rest. But being on your own does not mean completely dropping the ball. Masturbating in sweatpants or using the same vibrator every single night is no way to live. If this sounds like you, buy a new sex toy (see page 148 for ideas), light a Diptyque candle, and switch up your go-to position for once. You wouldn't want to have boring sex with another person, so why have it with yourself?

Things do get exponentially complicated when you introduce relative strangers into your sexual repertoire. You have to consider their feelings, wear nice underwear, and figure out who gets custody of the elevator when your fling ultimately fizzles out. But at the outset of every new sexual relationship, there are only three possible outcomes:

1. **THE SEX IS GOOD.**
2. **THE SEX IS BAD BECAUSE YOUR PARTNER LACKS SKILL.**
3. **THE SEX IS MEDIOCRE BECAUSE YOU AREN'T SEXUALLY COMPATIBLE.**

We don't talk enough about the third outcome. You could have incredible chemistry with someone, but that does not guarantee that the zsa zsa zsu will extend to the bedroom. Kissing is a good early indicator, but it is not a foolproof method of determining sexual rapport. Unlike partners who lack skill, sexual compatibility can be much harder to pinpoint because we often try to justify it. The sex may be a little underwhelming, but they're attractive and you're that couple that makes other couples in restaurants jealous. That must count for something, right? Not necessarily. Contrary to popular belief, hot people can be exceptionally boring lays. Conversely, you could have the best sex of your life with someone who you weren't attracted to initially, or as Anthony Marentino succinctly stated, "ugly sex is hot." We're not saying that you should find the most unfortunate-looking person on Tinder and swipe right. We're merely stating that attraction is not indicative of chemistry. If you don't believe us, just look at Charlotte's first—and second—marriage.

The spectrum of sexual expression is far more vast than *Sex and the City* would lead you to believe. Having sex in the missionary position with your bra on is great and all, but one must occasionally fuck outside the box. It is up to every Miranda to define her own particular erotic proclivities and carnal no-go areas. For example, you may be down to have phone sex, but it must be monogamous. Anilingus might be something that you're willing to try, but you need to be on the receiving end. Being open to trying new things is important, but not at the expense of your boundaries. When you are able to decode what makes you tick sexually (and what doesn't) it then becomes easier to find someone who is on the same page. Not everyone will share your freaky desires—but someone out there will. And others will discover that they are weirdly turned on by a Secret Service–themed roleplay scenario once you finally broach the subject with them. Finding a partner who you can effectively communicate with is a foundational element of a fulfilling sex life. We spend enough time censoring ourselves in our day-to-day life, so we shouldn't have to mince words with the person we're fucking. Mirandas require the very best in the bedroom, so it's up to you to keep your lovers in the loop. But if they happen to think that your clitoris is two inches away from its true location, it's time to abandon ship.

The Different Kinds of Sex

NOT ALL SEX IS CREATED EQUAL

AFFAIR SEX It may be morally reprehensible, but affair sex is undeniably hot. As Samantha once said, "They designed it that way." This kind of sex is so good that people are willing to jeopardize their marriages for the fleeting high of an erotic encounter. Unsurprisingly, affair sex is never sustainable. Someone always ends up getting their heart broken—or falling down a flight of stairs and chipping a tooth.

BAD SEX We've all had it. Whether you're sleeping with a person who is terrible in bed or someone who you aren't super attracted to, bad sex is a harrowing nightmare. It can be boring, depressing, gross, or all of the above. Bad sex feels like a punishment from the Universe, and being regularly subjected to it takes a major toll on your mental health. Your best bet is to flee to the safety of your Hitachi Magic Wand.

HATE SEX In theory, having sex with someone that you're mad at should be an aggravating and unpleasant experience, but in actuality, it's super fucking hot. Hate sex is all about playing with power dynamics and using the act of sex as a stand-in for an argument. It is rough by nature and often vaguely fucked up—see Carrie and Big's argument-turned-affair in season three.

GOOD SEX Good sex can take many forms and can occur with a wide range of partners. You could have good sex with a complete stranger or a significant other that you've slept with hundreds of times. There is no rhyme or reason when it comes to good sex, and sometimes the source of your orgasms can surprise you. Take Charlotte's unexpected rendezvous with Harry in season five. She wasn't feeling him initially, but they had good sex nonetheless.

OBLIGATORY SEX It's not quite as harrowing as bad sex, but it's not great either. Obligatory sex typically occurs in a long-term relationship, when the spark has faded but you still have to make an effort to sexually satisfy your partner (think Miranda and Steve in the first *Sex and the City* film). The only thing you can do is lie back, go through the motions, and think about fucking someone else so you can climax.

EX SEX Ex sex is convenient, but do not disregard the emotional minefield that you have chosen to walk into. As Samantha said, "If the sex is good, you don't have it anymore, and if it's bad—you just had sex with an ex." Ex sex rarely ends well, so unless a reconciliation is on the horizon, it's best to avoid it altogether.

LOVE SEX This is the hottest kind of sex, hands down. Nothing beats having great sexual chemistry with someone that you actually care about. Hate sex and affair sex may be hot, but they have a toxic, self-destructive quality that love sex does not. Love sex allows you to be truly intimate with another human being, which may or may not scare the shit out of you.

WE SHOULD ALL BE MIRANDAS

Nevertheless, She Persisted . . . to Masturbate

Life is stressful, so why not masturbate as often as humanly possible? Self-pleasure does wonders for your mental health *and* gives your cheeks a rosy glow that no amount of NARS blush can provide. It's a built-in coping mechanism for long workdays, bad dates, and horrifying *New York Times* push notifications. One can always fall back on masturbation in times of crisis, especially if you're a single girl who doesn't know where her next orgasm is coming from. Even if you do have a partner, it's never wise to abandon solo sex entirely. Your erotic imagination is yours and yours alone. Taking a moment to reconnect with yourself sexually should benefit your sex life, not hurt it. Just make sure that your partner takes priority over a back issue of *Jugs*.

How to Get Yourself Off in a New York Minute

SIX SEXUAL AIDS THAT EVERY
MIRANDA SHOULD OWN

Hitachi Magic Wand
This Samantha-approved device
is the Rolls Royce of vibrators.
Known for its incredibly strong
vibrations, the Hitachi has been a
reliable source of clitoral orgasms
since its debut in 1968.

Coconut Oil
Coconut oil is the best lubricant,
hands down. You can't use it with
condoms because like all oil-based
lubes, it can cause breakage
in latex, but for masturbatory
purposes, it's perfect—*and* it
doubles as a fabulous moisturizer.

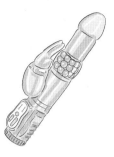

The Rabbit
Hype aside, the Rabbit is a legitimately good vibrator. It's perfect for women who can't climax from penetration alone . . . which, let's face it, is most of us.

Njoy Wand
Are you a squirter? You will know for sure after using this legendary dildo which was designed with g-spot orgasms in mind.

Butt Plug
You may or may not have an interest in butt plugs, but you *must* try one at least once to know where you stand.

Laptop
Watching porn on a desktop computer is awkward, and vaguely Skipper-ish. You *need* a laptop to bridge that gap between your desk and your bed. Just make sure to close those unsightly pop-ups after you climax.

People You Should

Definitely Not Fuck

YOUR STANDARDS ARE LOW—BUT NOT THIS LOW

1. People with lower self-esteem than you

2. People who live in your building

3. People who can't fuck you to save their life

4. People you work with

5. People with children you don't like

6. People in relationships

7. People who are addicted
to porn

8. People who take a shit with
the door open

9. People who go to your
Weight Watchers meeting

10. People named Skipper

Sometimes You Should
Fake an Orgasm

Third-wave feminism dictates that faking an orgasm is never a good idea. It gives your partner unrealistic expectations about how your body works, so they never have an opportunity to refine their technique. It can also lead you down a dark path of compulsive orgasm-faking. Once you start, you then have to maintain the illusion that you are a Samantha Jones—esque cum queen. If you stop faking, your partner may become suspicious and question the authenticity of your previous climaxes. Thereby, faking then becomes a vicious cycle that reinforces your partner's shitty lovemaking skills and leaves you feeling sexually unsatisfied.

Nothing good can come from compulsive faking, but *casual* faking? That's a completely different story. Casual faking is a get-out-of-jail free card for awkward, lackluster sexual situations. It's a choice that enables you to get randoms out of your bed-room in a timely fashion. Fake orgasms should typically be reserved for people that you don't really know and who you don't plan on fucking again. It's less about stroking their ego and more about getting an extra hour of sleep before that big meeting. They are not something to employ with people you're serious about dating, although sometimes granting a mercy orgasm is necessary. Take Miranda Hobbes's underwhelming sexual experience with an ophthalmologist in season two. He was listening to her directives and making a genuine attempt to satisfy her, but she knew that it would never happen. She faked an orgasm out of compassion—for both parties. Mirandas have too much on their plates to waste time having mediocre sex or running seminars on how to get a woman off. So, when the situation calls for it, just cut your losses and fake it.

Coloring Outside the Lines:
The Miranda's Guide to Fetishes

Fetishes! We all have them. For Ms. Hobbes, it was Betty Crocker and British soap operas about interracial couples. For you, it could be any number of freaky things that would horrify your mother. Broadly speaking, fetishes are sexual desires that are attached to a particular sex act, way of dress, part of the body, or mind-set. Even though *Sex and the City* had "sex" in the title and an (alleged) sexpert as its lead character, it lacked nuance when it came to fetishes. Whether it was Miranda's disturbed reaction to the prospect of reciprocal anilingus or Carrie publicly kink-shaming her politician boyfriend, the ladies rarely deviated from their limited sexual worldview. That is, everyone except Samantha, who was a beacon of sex-positivity in her relatively vanilla clique.

What turns people on sexually is as eclectic as Carrie's season two style. Every Miranda has her own sexual quirks and finding out what they are can be an extremely gratifying process. While one shouldn't partake in fetishes that disturb you, the Miranda-identified also shouldn't shun a fetish because of societal attitudes about what is and isn't degrading. Sexual acts and kinks that you're curious about are worth exploring, especially when you find a partner whose deviant preoccupations match yours. Fetishes should be thought of like accessorizing: a little will spice things up and a lot is a lifestyle choice.

Assplay The sexual practice of stimulating the buttocks and/or anus with one's mouth, finger(s), or penetration from a penis or sex toy.

Breathplay The restriction of oxygen, often during the act of sex, to heighten the intensity of an orgasm. Done by a partner it is referred to as erotic asphyxiation. The act by oneself is known as autoerotic asphyxiation.

BDSM An acronym for the practice of Bondage and Discipline [B/D], Dominance and Submission [D/s], and Sadomasochism [S/M]. Bondage refers to constricting a partner's limbs through restraints (handcuffs, ropes), while discipline is about punishment, whether physically (i.e., whipping) or mentally (i.e., orgasm denial). Dominance and Submission is a power dynamic exchange where the submissive gives control of their body and pleasure to a dominant. Sadomasochism is the exchange of physical and emotional pain, with the sadist finding pleasure in inflicting pain and the masochist deriving pleasure from being in pain.

CBT An acronym for "cock and ball torture," the practice of inflicting pain on a man's genitals for the purpose of sexual gratification.

Consensual Nonconsent This is a sex act performed wherein the participants consent to a roleplay scenario that mimics a nonconsensual sex act.

Cuckold A form of mental humiliation wherein a partner, usually a man, derives sexual gratification from their wife or girlfriend having sex with someone else in their presence. Not to be confused with Swinging or Threesomes.

Dirty Talk Speaking about sex acts or your partner in an obscene way as a form of foreplay or during intercourse.

Edging When a person is brought to the brink of orgasm, either alone or by a partner, but is stopped before reaching climax. This is said to increase the intensity once an orgasm is allowed. Also known as orgasm denial or orgasm control.

Exhibitionism Deriving sexual pleasure from exposing one's self in a public context and/or engaging in sexual acts in a public setting.

FemDom Wherein a female is the dominant partner, often engaging in BDSM-related scenes including but not limited to verbal humiliation, pegging, and bondage. Female dominants can be dominatrixes, but it is not a requirement.

Food Play The incorporation of food into foreplay and/or sex acts to enhance sexual gratification.

Foot Fetish An attraction to or sexual interest in feet.

Financial Domination A power exchange dynamic where the financial submissive gives gifts and/or money to their dominant (usually a female) willingly or through verbal humiliation.

Impact Play A sexual play act where the bottom or submissive is struck multiple times with an object (hand, riding crop, whip, flogger) by a top or their dominant for the sexual pleasure of one or both participating.

Medical Fetish A role play scenario in which objects, practices, or environments related to medical practices are used.

Mummification Wrapping of the body with rubber, plastic, or latex to confine movement and limit sensory perceptions (sight and sound).

Pony Play Roleplaying in which one acts as a human pony or owner of said human pony.

Rope Bondage A form of roleplaying where ropes are used to constrain movement for erotic pleasure.

Rough Sex Outside the realm of vanilla sex, anything that involves wild, vigorous, and kinky sex.

Sensation Play Using objects (flogger, velvet, ice) to create different sensations (not pain) on the skin to arouse.

Verbal Humiliation A psychological form of erotic humiliation wherein the participant is verbally demeaned for sexual arousal.

Voyeurism Deriving sexual pleasure from watching others engage in sex acts.

Watersports Any play that involves urine (drinking it, playing with it, peeing on someone). Also known as "golden showers."

Wax Play Dripping wax from a candle onto someone's body for erotic gratification.

WE SHOULD ALL BE MIRANDAS

Sext Like a Miranda

HOW TO SEND NUDES WITH DIGNITY

One of the most significant developments in dating since *Sex and the City* went off the air is the advent of sexting. Giving good sext is a crucial component of modern courtship, and it's something that tends to divide the Miranda-identified. Some of us love being able to plot our post-work fuck session down to the last dirty, disgusting detail, while others are repelled by the prospect of vocalizing their desires. Many Mirandas also feel burdened by the pressure to deliver well-composed (but not *too* staged-looking) nudes. Trying to find the optimal angle to photograph your naked body can easily trigger a meltdown, especially when you have to contend with unfortunate public restroom lighting. But the biggest downside of sexting is the potential for awkwardness and embarrassment—two things Mirandas typically avoid. Your partner could be repelled by your deviant sexual interests or you could wind up on a revenge porn website—and yet this invasive practice has become an expected part of dating.

Sending sexts may be taxing, but receiving them can be equally fraught. An unsolicited dick pic can pop up when you least expect it, and let's face it, most of them leave something to be desired. A sext with bad grammar is equally cringe-inducing, not to mention a total boner-killer.

In these moments, it's important to remember that you shouldn't be *too* critical. This is about sex—not syntax. Sexting is a safe way to let your imagination run wild and find out if your partner has any interest in that schoolgirl roleplay scenario that you've been keeping on the backburner. And yes, in a post-Kardashian world, a little paranoia is certainly merited, but as long as you crop out your face and aren't planning on running for Congress, it's unlikely that your blurry tit pics will end up on the front page of the *New York Star*.

Clear Your Browser History: The Miranda's Guide to Pornography

Mirandas tend to have a complicated relationship with pornography. On one hand, they occasionally enjoy the voyeuristic pleasure of watching two, or three, or even ten people having sex. On the other hand, they have a low tolerance for bad spray tans, overstuffed leather sofas, and ill-advised facial hair. Miranda Hobbes also had the added trauma of dating a man who preferred watching porn to having real-life sex with her. However, if you can find it in your heart to look past the harrowing aspects of Internet smut— and oh, there are many—porn can be a deeply satisfying sexual outlet. So if you're ready and willing to navigate this vast digital hellscape, here are the essential strategies that every Miranda should know.

BE SPECIFIC It can be painful to spell out your desires—especially if they aren't entirely politically correct—but specificity is the key to finding what you want in a timely fashion. If you aren't privy to the lexicon of popular search terms, a quick Google search for "porn acronyms" will enlighten you.

DIVERSIFY YOUR SMUT The porn that you watch doesn't necessarily need to reflect the kind of sex that you want in the real world. For example, a lot of lesbians enjoy watching gay male porn and many straight women enjoy watching lesbian porn. Don't feel restricted to the category that your IRL sex life fits into.

LOOK PAST THE GROSSNESS If you're going to watch porn, you're going to inevitably see things that you would prefer not to. For every video that you actually care to watch, there are ten super gross, quasi-disturbing videos that you have to weed through on your journey to pornographic fulfillment. Try not to be discouraged by the hunt.

WHEN IN DOUBT, SUBSCRIBE The only way to completely protect yourself from the aforementioned grossness is to find a specific kind of pornography that you like and subscribe to a website that only produces that kind of content. It is an added expense, but it saves you time and shields you from the countless horrors of Pornhub.

YOU ALWAYS HAVE OPTIONS If you genuinely can't get off on porn that caters to the male gaze—which is basically all of it—you do have other options. Most porn websites have a women's category, which tends to feature videos that are devoid of violence and extreme close-ups. You can also watch solo videos, which are inherently free of creepy, gendered power dynamics, or you can take a cue from Generation Z and get your pornography fix via NSFW gifs on Reddit instead.

FEELING DISGUSTED AFTERWARD IS NORMAL In fact, if you're not horrified by the video that you are watching the *second* after you climax, it probably isn't very good. Post-porn shame is an integral part of the experience. It doesn't make you a creepy pervert. On the contrary, it means that you are still a human being who is not completely desensitized to the dark recesses of the internet. The truly creepy perverts don't even think what they're watching is fucked up. So don't lose sleep over your browsing history! Remember, it's what gets you off, not who you are.

What's Your Name Again?

HOW TO BUILD A LASTING RELATIONSHIP FROM A ONE-NIGHT STAND

When is the right time to sleep with someone for the first time? Conventional wisdom (a.k.a. the Charlottes of the world) would say after the third date. Commonly known as the *Three-Date Rule,* this is the practice of waiting until the third date to have sex. This strategy is predicated on the belief that if you have sex with someone too quickly, it will hinder your ability to build a lasting relationship. The guiding principle behind this logic is that if your suitor thinks that you're slutty, they will deem you unworthy of a long-term relationship. With that in mind, here's something to contemplate: *you don't want to date that asshole anyway.* Furthermore, it shouldn't take you three dates to *know* whether you want to sleep with someone or not. If the attraction isn't there, don't subject yourself to multiple dates with some Richard Wright–esque monster.

Another thing to consider is that you don't want to wait three dates to discover that you and your love interest are sexually incompatible. A core conceit of the Three-Date Rule is that by getting to know someone first, the sex is guaranteed to be good. This is a lie. You don't need multiple dates to find this out; you actually need zero dates. God forbid that you wait to have sex, only to discover that your date is a terrible lay. Then you are faced with a horrible dilemma: break up with them now and risk looking selfish or keep dating them in the hopes that the sex will improve. And guess what? It won't. If you have bad sex the first time, you will have bad sex the second, the third, and the hundredth time. Good chemistry cannot be acquired, so even if you genuinely connect with the person or feel a strong attraction to them, your sexual dynamic is unlikely to improve.

Instead of the Three-Date Rule, perhaps we should consider the *No-Date Rule*. Contrary to popular belief, one-night stands are actually an ideal foundation for a long-term relationship. You can tell a lot about someone's character in the immediate aftermath of an impromptu sexual encounter. Some will kick you out of their bed and never text you again. Others will make you breakfast and walk you to work in the morning. Employing the No-Date Rule saves time while maximizing your orgasm potential. There are few things more erotic to a Miranda than optimal time management. To those of you who are still skeptical about this somewhat slutty approach to dating, just remember how Miranda and Steve met.

Anatomy of a Bedside Drawer

The contents of a woman's bedside drawer are like a window into her psyche. Don't fill yours with discarded condom wrappers and a well-worn Rabbit from 1998. Maintaining a well-stocked drawer of bedroom essentials is a crucial component of sexual self-care. Whether you're having sex with a partner or jerking off to the memory of your evil ex, it's important to have everything you need within arm's reach.

1. **LUBE.** You're an adult now: it's time to accept the fact that lube is essential, not optional. And don't even *think* about using shitty lube. That means no Astroglide, no K-Y Jelly, and no drugstore brands—period.

2. **CONDOMS.** If your sex life involves a penis, you'll probably need a stash of condoms to ward off STIs and/or pregnancy because, let's face it, you've slept with some questionable people.

3. **VIBRATOR.** Masturbating with your hand is an activity for people with lots of free time, which you just don't have. Vibrators are far more efficient—just be sure to play the field before making a lifelong commitment.

4. **WIPES.** Sex is gross and messy, which is why having prepackaged wipes or a soft cloth on hand is of the utmost importance. Your Ralph Lauren sheets will thank you.

"

I only give head to get head.

"

Three's a Crowd

HOW TO SURVIVE A THREESOME

We get it: threesomes are hot. But if you're thinking about having one, *proceed with extreme caution.* Theoretically, one should be able to have a fun, no-strings-attached sexual encounter with a new partner (or two), but under the wrong circumstances, a threesome can quickly lead to jealousy, trust issues, and a host of soul-crushing drama that will quickly compel you to flee to the safety of monogamy—or possibly celibacy. Not everyone is capable of having group sex without complicating their relationships, so it's imperative that you accurately assess the potential risks of all parties involved before it gets messy.

If you're having a three-way, you are either one half of a very sexually adventurous couple, or what Samantha refers to as the "guest star." Being a guest star is the best possible scenario in a threesome, because you get to have all of the fun without having to navigate the ins and outs of nonmonogamy. The emotional stakes are low for a guest star, although you do have to make sure that you aren't harboring romantic feelings for either partner before entering into such an arrangement. Fucking a fabulous person who is already committed is like fondling a handbag with a five-year wait-list. No orgasm is worth this kind of pain. Conversely, if either half of the couple should develop feelings for you, do know it's acceptable to ghost them. After all, getting in, getting off, and getting the fuck *out* is the guest star's job. Don't overstay your welcome.

Entering a three-way as part of a couple requires a bit more forethought. Is jealousy an issue in your relationship? Have you had troubles with fidelity? Is the guest star the kind of person who might stalk both of you? All of these questions need to be answered in advance, because Mirandas don't have time for some *Single White Female*-type bullshit. You and your partner must be on the same page from the get-go, and that includes a discussion about how you are going to conduct yourselves during and after the encounter. Are certain sex acts off-limits with the guest star? Will you continue to communicate with him or her after the fact? This should go without saying, but unless you are a seasoned polyamorist, fucking the same guest star repeatedly is ill-advised. Additionally, you must consider your *proximity* to the guest star. Strangers and acquaintances make great guest stars, whereas friends and neighbors do not.

Generally speaking, you can almost always tell if a three-way is a bad idea from the outset. For example, Samantha's decision to sleep with a gay male couple was obviously a horrible idea. Same goes for her ill-advised romp with Richard Wright and a much younger woman who she was clearly threatened by. In situations like this, you have to let your intuition—not your libido—call the shots. Thinking with your genitals will only lead to unnecessary drama, and you deserve more than that. Group sex is one of life's great pleasures, but it should be used sparingly, like Chanel No. 5. Don't fuck yourself into a corner.

The Wisdom of Samantha

She is the resident sexpert of Lower Manhattan. The originator of "dickalicious." The Michiko Kakutani of vibrators. And unlike Carrie, she *actually* knows good sex. Samantha Jones has spent countless hours on her back, her knees, and in a rooftop pool while Sade is playing. She has survived sex swings, pearl thongs, and Mr. Too Big.

Let Samantha's epic journey inspire you to expand your horizons, get flexible, and ditch that loser that you shouldn't bother fucking.

I'M A TRY-SEXUAL. I'LL TRY ANYTHING ONCE You only live once, so why not urinate on someone while you can? We all develop a sexual repertoire that we feel confident in—and at times, fall back on. While feeling comfortable during sex is certainly crucial, it's equally important to be open to new things. Without experimentation, you'll never know about all of the weird stuff that you're surprisingly cool with doing in bed.

FUCK ME BADLY ONCE, SHAME ON YOU. FUCK ME BADLY TWICE, SHAME ON ME There is nothing more tragic than having boring, mediocre sex when you could be at home using your favorite dildo instead. Could it be a fluke fuck? Sure. But do you really want to take that risk? After one bad lay, the Universe has spoken: you're not sexually compatible. If you choose to go back for more, you have no one to blame but yourself.

SOMETIMES YOU JUST NEED A BIG COCK Yes, size does matter. Many women downplay the importance of size because they are chained to the same dick day in and day out. They typically say that they're fine with anything that isn't monstrously big or shockingly small, but there are times when one simply *requires* an above-average cock—which is where dildos come in. If you don't have a well-endowed partner, dildos are a fabulous alternative because you can have the dick of your dreams without the added burden of the person attached to it. If you don't already own one, put down this book and go shopping immediately.

A BAD KISSER IS A NON-NEGOTIABLE Kissing is a good and early indication whether you'll have chemistry with a person between the sheets. A lack of technique is a huge red flag. If they have not mastered the simple art of tongue-on-tongue action, they are unlikely to fare better when they venture below the belt. The best course of action is to fake a stomach bug and ghost them.

WHO WE ARE IN BED IS WHO WE ARE IN LIFE Can you be a terrible lay, but a great person? Samantha Jones would say no. She believes that how we behave in the world is indicative of how we conduct ourselves during sex—and vice versa. An egotistical and unimaginative person will probably be a selfish and boring lover, so pay close attention to your lover's behavior, both in (and out) of the bedroom.

Your Fuck List

HOW MANY IS TOO MANY?

Miranda Hobbes felt that she had a few too many notches on her bedpost, but we're here to tell you that there is nothing wrong with having a large (or small) number of sexual partners. Who you choose to sleep with is no one's business but your own. (Although it is advisable to keep a list of their names in the event of an STD diagnosis.)**

1. _____
2. _____
3. _____
4. _____
5. _____
6. _____
7. _____
8. _____
9. _____
10. _____
11. _____
12. _____
13. _____
14. _____
15. _____
16. _____
17. _____
18. _____
19. _____
20. _____
21. _____
22. _____
23. _____
24. _____
25. _____
26. _____
27. _____
28. _____
29. _____
30. _____
31. _____
32. _____
33. _____
34. _____
35. _____
36. _____
37. _____
38. _____
39. _____
40. _____

41. _____   71. _____
42. _____   72. _____
43. _____   73. _____
44. _____   74. _____
45. _____   75. _____
46. _____   76. _____
47. _____   77. _____
48. _____   78. _____
49. _____   79. _____
50. _____   80. _____
51. _____   81. _____
52. _____   82. _____
53. _____   83. _____
54. _____   84. _____
55. _____   85. _____
56. _____   86. _____
57. _____   87. _____
58. _____   88. _____
59. _____   89. _____
60. _____   90. _____
61. _____   91. _____
62. _____   92. _____
63. _____   93. _____
64. _____   94. _____
65. _____   95. _____
66. _____   96. _____
67. _____   97. _____
68. _____   98. _____
69. _____   99. _____
70. _____

** If you are in triple digits, no judgment! You have a healthy sexual appetite, but a Google spreadsheet may be better suited to your needs.

What I Hate in Life, I Love in Sex

If you don't remember Miranda Hobbes stating, "What I hate in life, I love in sex," it's probably because you were too distracted by the fact that she was wearing a bucket hat *over* a hooded windbreaker when she uttered those words. Let's not allow a questionable fashion choice to overshadow what is arguably her most profound statement about sexuality, though. Miranda was referencing a date with a macho lawyer who made a habit of bossing her around in and out of the bedroom. She lamented that she hated his controlling behavior in her everyday life, but loved it in her sex life. On the surface, this seems like a paradox, but when you look deeper, the true logic of Miranda's statement becomes clear.

Our culture has never been particularly kind to women. We're expected to tolerate a host of sexist microaggressions, like mansplaining and manspreading, while also coping with the pervasive reality of discrimination and sexual assault. Every woman handles the reality of misogyny differently, and for some that includes eroticizing the sexist behavior that permeates the culture around them. Lots of women want to be bossed around by a dominant partner, à la Miranda. Others enjoy verbal degradation, rough sex, or even a full-fledged masked intruder roleplay scenario like Samantha experienced in season six. Enjoying any or all of these things doesn't make you a creepy pervert— it makes you a human being trying to make sense of a deeply fucked-up world. Do yourself a favor, and lean in to your darker impulses. You never know—there might be a secret sadist or bossy bottom lurking just below your surface.

WHAT YOU SHOULD HAVE
LEARNED FROM THIS CHAPTER

- One-night stands are great first dates.
- Sexual compatibility is everything.
- Self-pleasure is not optional.
- Clear your browser history.
- There is no such thing as too much lube.
- Don't fuck your neighbor.
- Threesomes can be messy.
- Your number is nothing to be ashamed of.
- Faking an orgasm is an act of mercy.
- The good ones fuck you, the bad ones fuck you, and the rest of them don't know how to fuck you.

CHAPTER 6

THRIVE LIKE A MIRANDA

Eat (Cake Out of
the Garbage), Pray, Love

Self-Care for Dummies

When Samantha screamed, "You hear that, New York? We have it all!" she wasn't wrong. Ms. Jones and her three cohorts all had cool jobs, fabulous apartments, and colorful sex lives. By the time the films rolled around, they had achieved virtually every personal and professional milestone imaginable, all while donning current-season Vuitton and Cavalli. But much like the Fendi baguette, the concept of "having it all" met its demise in the new millennium. Women wisely realized that most of us could *never* have it all. Having a great career, a perfect marriage, a plush bank account, and Kim Cattrall's good genes are privileges that are afforded to few.

The majority of us have to learn to thrive in the absence of these things, not because of them.

One could argue that the booming wellness industry is a direct response to the end of the "having it all" myth. When our hopes and ambitions fail to materialize, a green juice becomes our only recourse. This approach is seemingly productive, but there is one major problem: Mirandas like to make fun of wellness. Jade rollers, vaginal steaming, and the Tracy Anderson Method are fodder for our snappy one-liners, not practices that we'd like to adopt. We don't want to treat ourselves like garbage, but we also don't want to buy into an industry that thrives on pseudoscience and crystals. Navigating the world of wellness can be triggering for Mirandas, but we must persevere nonetheless. Some of it is bullshit—but not all of it is bullshit. Cobbling together a sustainable self-care practice is your responsibility, and yours alone. You can hate the term "self-care practice" all you want, but do not disregard its importance. Thriving like a Miranda means cultivating an approach to living that makes it possible to exist in the world without being completely fucking miserable. Nothing is off-limits.

Maintaining your physical and emotional health is critical to your ability to flourish. Resigning yourself to being sad and anemic is not flourishing, although that succinctly describes most winters that we've had. The endless flurry of work and social obligations can easily distract us from our basic needs—however, being busy is not an excuse. If you refuse to prioritize your health over your "rise-and-grind" lifestyle, you can't expect to thrive. Exercise, adequate sleep, a semihealthy diet, and regular contact with loved ones is a requirement for everyone, not an option. Mirandas with mental health issues must be especially diligent about taking care of themselves. Failure to actively manage a condition like depression can negatively affect your sleep, diet, will to live, etc. But even if you don't suffer from mental health issues, adhering to a healthy lifestyle can be challenging. Many of us have issues and vices that inhibit us from making great decisions all the time. All we can do is actively commit to bettering our lives and managing our self-sabotaging behavior to the best of our ability. The key to thriving is tenacity, not perfection. Don't be discouraged if you fuck up from time to time.

We hate to say it, but you need to develop a spiritual practice, too. If you're cringing already: we get it. Mirandas are often resistant to anything that is tangentially related to religion or seems excessively bohemian, but as many of you already know, spirituality is not limited to those who attend mass or conduct ayahuasca ceremonies. Every person on this earth is inherently spiritual (except for Anthony Marentino, who has a black hole where his soul should be). You don't have to pray, renounce your sins, or protest outside of an abortion clinic to be spiritual. You don't even have to like meditation. All you have to do is cultivate a routine that makes you feel detached from your own petty bullshit and connected to the greater world around you. For many, spending time in nature does the trick. Others feel connected when they're at church, twelve-step meetings, or at home watching YouTube videos of Oprah. Your approach doesn't have to be like anyone else's, and it certainly doesn't have to involve a gratitude jar. That said, make an effort to remain open-minded. When a Miranda steps outside of her comfort zone, her first instinct is to be sarcastic, but this is precisely why we need spirituality the most. Looking beyond ourselves is the only thing that can rescue us from the toxic depths of our own cynicism. It's up to you to find a routine that doesn't make you judge yourself.

Thriving like a Miranda isn't about having a perfect life, it's about making the best of an imperfect one. We will always have moments—scratch that—*years* where we feel lost, scared, or downright miserable, but if we make a conscious effort to take care of ourselves, we can endure them. A spa treatment or a hot yoga class will not solve our problems, but these small gestures are powerful reminders that we do care about ourselves. Self-care provides us with strength, self-worth, and a temporary distraction from the shitshow that we call life. We may never have it all, but at least we can buy a sheet mask.

SUGGESTED SELF-CARE PRACTICES

Throw your phone in the ocean

Back up your computer

Spend an entire day masturbating

Buy an obscenely expensive candle

Beat someone with a bouquet of flowers

Read a fucking book

Look at your pores in a magnifying mirror

Eat an entire box of Double Stuf Oreos

Reconnect with nature

Reconnect with your pot dealer

Have phone sex

Burn your skinny jeans

Buy every single tabloid at the grocery store

Throw a drink in someone's face

Take a napa

Move to Napa

Rearrange your furniture

Get a Brazilian

Listen to "a hell of a lot of Sinatra"

Have a purse party

Go to the gym

Pick someone up at the gym

Get a manicure

Evolve your look

Purge your closet

Call your fuck buddy

Eat Like a Miranda

Ever since "wellness" has usurped "dieting" as the new weight loss buzzword, no Miranda can eat her Seamless order in peace. Diets, while cruel and unusual, were at least temporary. Eating healthy is now a full-time job, and the expectation that we should dine like Gwyneth (a Charlotte) 24/7 is only setting us up for failure. Temporarily adopting this lifestyle will only lead to the compulsive overeating of baked goods—and the inevitable shame spiral that follows. We cannot deprive ourselves of complex carbohydrates indefinitely, but we also can't give into all of our worst food instincts. In this new, terrifying landscape of matcha lattes and poke bowls, what is a Miranda to do?

A far more realistic and achievable eating philosophy is what we call the 75/25 Diet™. Seventy-five percent of your diet is composed of healthy foods, like vegetables, legumes, and lean protein, and the other 25 percent is reserved for complete and utter garbage. Buffalo wings, spring rolls, and Krispy Kremes are all foods that you can comfortably indulge in—but only a quarter of the time. It's far from a perfect science, but it's better than that vicious cycle of dieting and overindulging.

THE 75/25 DIET

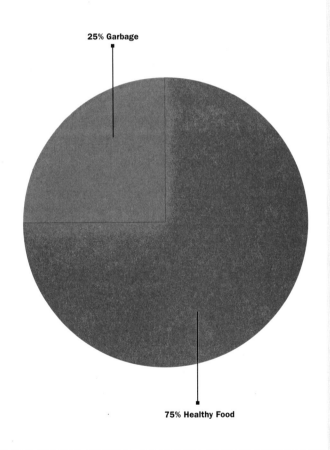

25% Garbage

75% Healthy Food

What the Fuck Should I Eat?

To succeed at the 75/25 Diet, you must resist the urge to eat crap *all* the time. We know that this doesn't come naturally to everyone, so we've created a list of healthy options that you can substitute for your favorite foods.

INSTEAD OF THIS . . .	TRY THIS!
Frappuccino	black coffee
PB&J	a handful of unsalted almonds
tacos	lettuce cups
ice cream	a single ice cube
pork lo mein	zoodles
clam chowder in a bread bowl	açai bowl
eggs Benedict	egg white omelet
a Magnolia cupcake	a vegan scone
steak	grilled tofu
Coca-Cola	LaCroix
potato chips	baked kale chips
carrot cake	a carrot
pizza	gluten-free bruschetta

"

I'm going to
find my inner
goddess
if it kills me.

"

Why Did We Stop Drinking These?

The most self-aware moment in the first *Sex and the City* film was when Miranda took a sip of her Cosmopolitan and asked her friends, "Why did we stop drinking these?" to which Carrie responded, "Because everyone else started." Like Magnolia cupcakes and Rabbit vibrators, *Sex and the City* created a nationwide craze for Cosmos. But when they fell out of fashion, they fell *hard*. No longer associated with chic, metropolitan women, Cosmos became the unofficial beverage of what we lovingly refer to as "the basic bitch." Today, the mere thought of a Cosmopolitan conjures up images of French manicures and regrettable bachelorette parties, but like all things passé, the Cosmo is primed for a comeback. No amount of pink feather boas can change the fact that it's still a legitimately good drink. So dust off your fake Fendi, grab your friends, and indulge in Carrie & Co.'s signature cocktail. Trust us—they're about to be cool again.

The No-Bullshit Cosmopolitan

INGREDIENTS

2 ounces vodka

1 ounce cranberry
juice cocktail

¾ ounce fresh lime
juice

¾ ounce triple sec

Lime wedge or orange
twist, for garnish

DIRECTIONS

Add all ingredients to
cocktail shaker with ice.
Shake vigorously until chilled.
Double-strain (from shaker
through fine-mesh strainer)
into chilled cocktail glass.
Garnish with a wedge of lime
or an orange twist. Enjoy
responsibly, or be doomed
to drunk dial your ex.

187

Work It Out

Shopping may be Carrie's cardio, but Miranda Hobbes was a true fitness devotee who ran marathons, lifted weights, and occasionally picked up men in the process. While many Mirandas enjoy exercise, this is by no means a universal trait. An equal number of us simply deplore it. For a fitness-adverse Miranda, the gym is the most triggering place of all: you have to sweat profusely in front of complete strangers, wear flip flops in the shower, and coexist with grunting gym rats. It's no surprise that many of us regularly pass up exercise in favor of happy hour. But even if you despise working out, you still have to do it. After all, forcing yourself to do shit that you hate is an important part of being an adult. Your health should take priority over your aversion to Planet Fitness, and the sooner you realize that, the better.

The simple act of getting to the gym, or a class, or wherever you burn your calories is half the battle. Most people bail on exercise at the last minute with a barely logical excuse, mentally rattling off justifications like "I'm tired," or "I need to work late," or "I forgot my gym socks." Having the ability to take a step back and observe your thoughts when your mind goes into "fuck it" mode is the best thing you can do to keep yourself on track. Occasionally, you will have a completely legitimate reason to skip your Pilates class, but more often than not, you will discover that you are making excuses that only benefit you in the short term. Don't fall for your own bullshit.

Finding a form of exercise that you don't totally hate is equally crucial. If you can't stand kickboxing, try yoga instead. If you dislike gyms, go hiking. A lot of people who hate exercise think that working out means treadmills, push-ups, and weightlifting, but your fitness regimen doesn't have to include any of that stuff. Maybe you prefer ballet or Cher's seminal aerobics videos. Perhaps you'd rather ride an actual bike than listen to the motivational musings of a SoulCycle instructor. It's impossible to sustain an exercise regimen that you despise, so don't commit to a sadistic military-themed workout just because it burns a thousand calories an hour. You'll inevitably flame out after a couple weeks and flee to the safety of your couch. The goal is to maintain a consistent workout routine that you can stick to for years. So find out what you like, pay no mind to the fads, and remember that showing up half of the time is so much better than not showing up at all.

Lunge Like a Miranda

Incorporating calisthenics into your morning routine is one of the easiest ways to keep your body fit and strong. These simple exercises are timeless, bullshit-free, and can be done practically anywhere, so put on NPR and devote ten minutes a day to the basics. You may not get Michelle Obama arms overnight, but good things will come to those who plank.

plank

sit-up

squat

lunge

Keep Calm and Charlotte On

Sarcasm is a Miranda's lifeblood. It allows us to show our contempt for people, institutions, and the world at large in a socially acceptable way. Wait, who are we kidding? It's an unproductive coping mechanism meant to mask a wide range of unpleasant emotions. Left unchecked, compulsive sarcasm can propel one into full-tilt cynicism. There is a fine line between the occasional well-timed barb and a chronically pessimistic outlook. Yes, sometimes it feels like everything is awful and *someone* has to make fun of it, but the goal is to make yourself feel better, not to make everyone in your orbit feel worse. What's a Miranda to do when her point of view starts to alienate those around her? Perhaps it's time to look on the bright side, for once. And if being hopeful does not come naturally to you, let the eternal optimist and Burberry enthusiast Charlotte York Goldenblatt be your guide.

For those who are sardonically inclined, optimism is a trait of the naive. These intellectually inferior halfwits are simply looking at the world through rose-colored glasses. It's worth noting, though, that Charlotte faced her fair share of hardships, including but not limited to divorce, miscarriage, and having Bunny MacDougal as an in-law. Yet despite her struggles, her optimism never wavered. Charlotte did not let her abysmal first marriage or the plethora of bad dates that followed dampen her search for true love. Her ability to see the best in every situation—even when she shouldn't have—was a conscious choice, not happenstance. Yes, some situations are impossible to see the good in, like some dude calling you a "fucking bitch" and a "fucking whore," but consciously fighting the urge to retreat into cynicism is more productive than letting it take control of you. The act of pessimism is an agreement with the world to no longer be present in it. To accept optimism into your life means being brave enough to be surprised. Charlotte knew that she wanted marriage and family, but she didn't know how she was going to get there. Her resolve brought her on a journey that saw her change faiths and open herself up to adoption. A more dour person would have given up around the time that Trey brought home a cardboard baby.

If abject optimism is just too much to ask, but you concede that cynicism is no way to live, maybe the best that any Miranda can do is to strive to be an optimistic cynic. The world is a dark, harrowing, fucked-up place, but seeing the positives when you can is what makes it bearable—and despite our claims to the contrary, there actually is a glass-is-half-full bitch trapped inside all of us. The sooner we embrace her, the better. So when you feel a cacophony of negative remarks starting to swirl around in your brain, take a pause and ask yourself, W.W.C.Y.G.D.?—What Would Charlotte York Goldenblatt Do?

THRIVE LIKE A MIRANDA

Depression Is a Bitch

THE MIRANDA'S GUIDE TO MENTAL HEALTH

Unfortunately, Mirandas are not immune to the basic bitches of mental disorders: depression and anxiety. Some people experience one or both of these afflictions in times of crisis. Others have to cope with these illnesses for life. Both scenarios are objectively awful. If your issues stem from a stressful, life-altering situation, take comfort in the fact that you won't feel like this forever. If you experience prolonged mental anguish for no apparent reason, well, then you're fucked. But while you may be fucked, you are by no means alone. Many Mirandas (and Carries, and Charlottes, and Samanthas) live with mental health issues, and as futile as things can seem when you're flailing around in the darkness, there is *always* something that you can do to pull yourself closer to the light. Trust us.

STAY FUCKING PRESENT Depression is pointless because it makes people dwell on past events they can't change or personal shortcomings that they could change if they weren't so depressed. Anxiety, on the other hand, is characterized by a fear of the future. People with anxiety analyze challenges that they face and use them to mentally construct horrifying future scenarios, which they then obsess over. Depression and anxiety are equally counterproductive because they take people out of the present moment, which is the only time that you can actually make positive changes in your life. If you're spiraling, try to ground yourself and focus on the small things that you can do *right now*.

PULL AN ELIZABETH TAYLOR After her miscarriage, Charlotte sought comfort in the life story of Elizabeth Taylor, a brilliant and impossibly glamorous actress whose private life was riddled with failed relationships, addiction, and mental illness. Despite her demons, Taylor soldiered on in her signature jewels and caftans, creating a prolific body of work and later finding a greater purpose as an AIDS activist. She didn't let setbacks and failures completely destroy her; she instead nourished herself with glamour and gave back to those around her. Every Miranda can learn a thing or two from her example.

LAY OFF THE COSMOS Or the chocolate cake, or the weed, or whatever your go-to vice is during times of stress. Numbing your emotions by overindulging to the point of self-destruction will never solve your problems. It only distracts you from them, while simultaneously creating new problems related to your addiction. Yes, sometimes exerting even an ounce of self-control can feel downright impossible for a Miranda who is in crisis, but all of us are capable of making small decisions that benefit us, even if it's just talking to a friend or therapist about what we're feeling.

DO THE RIGHT THINGS Mirandas tend to be very attentive to their careers and relationships with others, but they often drop the ball when it comes to taking care of themselves. If you suffer from mental health issues, you have to do all of the stuff that you would tell a friend to do. You have to see a doctor, and in some instances, take medication. You have to exercise and eat right. You have to get eight hours of sleep and cultivate mindfulness practices. Your self-destructive side will routinely try to sabotage you, but you must persevere in spite of it. And you can.

PROGRESS ISN'T LINEAR Like any chronic illness, mental health issues tend to recur with varying degrees of severity throughout one's life. You may work hard to pull yourself out a dark period, only to promptly fall flat on your face again. Mental health issues require a lifetime of self-management. Don't get discouraged if you stumble, relapse, or have a panic attack on the street like Miranda Hobbes did after she bought her first apartment. Low points are inevitable, but they do not negate all the of the hard work that you have done. You may be fucking crazy, but you're stronger than you think.

Your Friends
Are Your Soulmates

Lovers come and go, but your friends are the bitches who you are trapped with *for life*. And thank God for that, because if we had to rely on people who fuck us for unconditional love and support, we'd probably die alone. The relationships that we cultivate with our friends are often the most gratifying of our lifetimes. They provide us with emotional intimacy, minus the bullshit that goes hand in hand with romance, or as Samantha so succinctly stated: "Men are for fucking, women are for friendship."

That said, not all friends are soulmates. Some friends come into our lives during a very specific period of time. Perhaps you develop a bond with a colleague that fizzles out after one of you gets a new job, or maybe you have a handful of party friends that slowly disappear as you outgrow your club-rat phase. Although fickle, ephemeral friendships are still valuable because they teach us about who we are, and often, who we no longer want to be. Charlotte found that out the hard way when she decided to reunite with her hyperconservative sorority sisters. After scandalizing them with the details of her sex life, she quickly learned that not all friendships are built to last—nor should they. Don't feel bad about outgrowing a relationship that no longer suits you. After all, your real friends would *love* to hear you drunkenly proclaim, "Sometimes I just need to be fucked!" in the middle of a crowded restaurant.

Unlike ephemeral friends, your soulmates are the people who show up for you no matter what. They will listen to you bitch about your evil ex for hours on end. They will throw you dignified, storkless baby showers complete with fried chicken per your request. They will voluntarily extract your diaphragm from your vagina should it become stuck. Okay, so maybe that last example is something that *only* happened on *Sex and the City*, but the sentiment behind this very specific occurrence is universal. Your soulmates will deal with gross, annoying shit on your behalf and you will do the same for them. Like 14th Street, friendship is a two-way street. You must both be attentive to each other's needs in order for things to work. Even if you hit the occasional snag—like a pretentious Russian boyfriend that one of you hates—you must make an effort to work through your differences. You might have to woo your soulmate with bagels, or resort to stalking if she stops answering your calls. But if you two are truly *bashert,* as Charlotte says, everything will work out in time. Soulmates are for life, so treat them with the love and respect that they deserve. And remember: never, *ever* settle for anything less than butterflies.

What's the Wi-Fi?

THE MIRANDA'S GUIDE TO TRAVEL

Traveling, while fabulous, can be an intense source of anxiety for the Miranda-identified. By definition, it requires us to leave the safety of our home base and plunge headfirst into the unknown, where we then become vulnerable to airborne viruses, faulty internet connections, and a host of other travel-related mishaps. Make no mistake, though, this chaos is a gift. Having the opportunity to visit different places and experience other cultures is a privilege that is not afforded to everyone. That said, not all travel is created equal.

Some of us have to travel for work, which is hardly a vacation because we still have to do our jobs, often from the comfort of a hotel room that we'd rather not be in. Others have to travel to visit family, which can be a nightmare if you hate your in-laws or the small midwestern town where they reside. These travel scenarios are not vacations; they are temporary relocations to a Marriott or a guest bedroom from hell. Real vacations involve poolside cocktails, breakfast buffets, and turndown service. If you're anything like Miranda Hobbes, these luxurious escapes are few and far between. Work and familial obligations often prevent us from traveling as much as we'd like, as do our finances. Many of us cannot consider vacations until we achieve the financial stability that (sometimes) comes with being older—but even if you're not planning a girls' trip to Abu Dhabi anytime soon, it's important to learn the basics of travel. You never know when you will be thrust outside of your comfort zone, but you'll want the right travel adapter when you get there.

VACATION DYSPHORIA IS NORMAL The key to being a Miranda on vacation is accepting that you're on vacation. Even if you planned it yourself, it can be difficult to detach from the pressures of everyday life. When combined with a healthy dose of jet lag, even the most travel-adept Mirandas can feel out of sorts. And that is okay. The anxiety that comes with not working is definitive proof that you *need a fucking vacation*, so take a deep breath, order a piña colada, and try to unplug to the best of your ability.

GETTING THERE WILL SUCK Visiting foreign lands is great and all, but in order to get there we must contend with flight delays, humiliating TSA practices, and a host of other transportation snafus. Expecting the worst is the *only* way to approach a long travel day. Do not delude yourself into thinking that everything will go smoothly. If your trip goes off without a hitch, great. But if it doesn't, at least you'll be prepared.

LEARN HOW TO CARRY ON Checking bags is for Carries. If you're going away for a long weekend, you should be able to function with a single carry-on bag. It may require you to do a bit of editing, but remember that nothing is more satisfying than bypassing baggage claim. You'll save money on fees *and* avoid unsightly scuffs on your new luggage.

INTERNATIONAL TRAVEL (THE BORING STUFF) Yes, getting that stamp on your passport is très chic, but there are a host of annoying details that require your attention beforehand. Did you know that in many countries, your passport is invalid if it expires in less than six months? And that some countries like Australia require you to apply for a tourist visa even if you're staying for less than ninety days? Also, be conscious of your phone usage. Nothing ruins the afterglow of a European vacation like realizing that your smartphone has been roaming for the last two weeks. Check your provider's international plans, or invest in a SIM card before your trip.

DON'T LEAVE THINGS IN THE SEAT-BACK POCKET This should be a no-brainer, but almost all of us have made this fatal mistake at one point or another. If you leave anything behind on an airplane, you are unlikely to see it ever again, so think before you store anything important in the seat-back pocket. Or at the very least, commit to doing an extremely thorough search before you deplane.

CHILL THE FUCK OUT Mirandas can be control freaks, so the unpredictable nature of travel can easily test our patience. But that doesn't mean that we should ruin things for everyone else. Freaking out when we miss a connecting flight or having work-related meltdowns when we should be relaxing is not fun for our travel companions. Be conscious of the fact that you are especially prone to becoming frazzled mess—and apologize accordingly.

PACK LIKE A MIRANDA

- Take the batteries out of your vibrator, or risk alerting the bomb squad.
- Pack a wide selection of shoes that you can actually walk in—and make sure to break them in *before* you leave.
- Leave space in your suitcase for the things that you will acquire on your trip, or be prepared to pay an overweight bag fee.
- Always pack one piece of outerwear that is slightly warmer than what you anticipate needing.
- Hotel irons are not to be trusted. Invest in a high-quality portable steamer instead.
- Create a travel-size version of your medicine cabinet. Trips to foreign drug stores can be fun, but having tampons, painkillers, and other essentials on hand will give you peace of mind if you're feeling less than stellar.
- Pull a Carrie, and keep a pashmina in your carry-on. They're less bulky than blankets and you can always wear them as a scarf should you need to free up extra room in your bag.
- Keep a portable charger on hand *at all times*. A delayed flight is bad, but a delayed flight without a phone is the second circle of hell.
- Pack that one item that you are debating taking, as it will inevitably become the most vital item of your vacation. Listen to your gut.

Put Down
Your Smartphone

If you're reading this, congratulations! You put down your phone long enough to read an actual book. Or at least part of a book, which is certainly more than most people can say these days. In less than two decades, portable phones have transformed almost every aspect of our lives. We work differently, shop differently, and stalk our exes differently. While convenient, this lightning-fast proximity to information has become an addiction. Many of us have become dependent on our phones with a fervor that was once reserved for drugs and alcohol. When we become separated from these devices, a perfectly sane Miranda can quickly devolve into a Carrie at the height of her Big affair. We've all read enough think-pieces to know that people who spend an excessive amount of time staring at screens are more likely to suffer from depression and anxiety, yet we are unable to modify our behavior, even when we want to.

Smartphones have become integral to modern working life, or at least that's the excuse we use to justify our reliance on them. Sure, they allow us to respond to work emails from the back seat of an Uber, but they have also turned us into content creation

monsters. Simple activities like going to dinner or spending a day at the beach have mutated into highly curated photoshoots, providing the poster an instant dopamine hit for each like received. The simple act of scrolling through a stranger's feed can easily incite jealousy, judgment, or straight-up misery. It also distracts us from what's happening right in front of us. If you find yourself more interested in an acquaintance's feed than the person sitting in front of you, it's time to consciously uncouple from your phone.

We would never suggest something as draconian as getting a flip-phone—no matter how chic Carrie's pink bedazzled one looked. No, forsaking Google Maps and Spotify isn't an option. However, a reprieve from the perpetual overstimulation is necessary, so put your fucking phone away—at least for a few hours. You will have to integrate this technology cleanse into your daily schedule, because you cannot be trusted to moderate your own behavior on the fly. When separated from your phone, especially for short bursts, you realize the world doesn't end when a text or email isn't promptly responded to. This simple practice will help retrain your brain to be present. Your friends will thank you, and anonymous restaurant patrons won't have to watch you photograph a chocolate tart for ten minutes. It's a public service, really.

If all else fails, watch *Sex and the City* reruns. In that dial-up world, Miranda's BlackBerry is the hottest piece of technology and Stanford is still cruising for sex in chat rooms. It's actually a miracle that this series existed in a pre–social media world, because if Carrie had the ability to see Natasha's Instagram, it might have killed her. Charlotte would be a Pinterest addict, Samantha would have an unhealthy relationship with Tinder, and Anthony would be a full-fledged Twitter troll. Thankfully, we were spared from these plotlines and can now find solace in a series that predates read receipts. *Sex and the City* has always been escapist television, but now, in addition to living vicariously through these glamorous women, we can escape from the burden of technology as well.

Wear Your
Fucking Sunscreen

... AND OTHER CRUCIAL BEAUTY TIPS

When it comes to beauty, a Miranda always errs on the side of minimalism. Hell, we're the reason Clinique was invented. Over-the-top makeup may work well on others (see: Carrie's season six statement blush), but on you, it will almost always look freakish. This is not to say that Mirandas lack technique in the beauty arena. After all, many of us know the ins and outs of liquid eyeliner. The problem lies with the fact that an overly contrived beauty look is incongruous with our no-nonsense nature, so when we go over-board, it's not just tacky—it's inauthentic, too. Furthermore, a maximalist approach is also not conducive to optimal time man-agement. A Charlotte may enjoy staring at her pores for hours on end, but Mirandas just don't have time for that shit. A less-is-more approach will free up countless hours, so you can spend more time on activities that you *do* enjoy, like drinking coffee, eating pies, having sex, and enjoying battery-operated devices.

Here's how to do beauty the Miranda way.

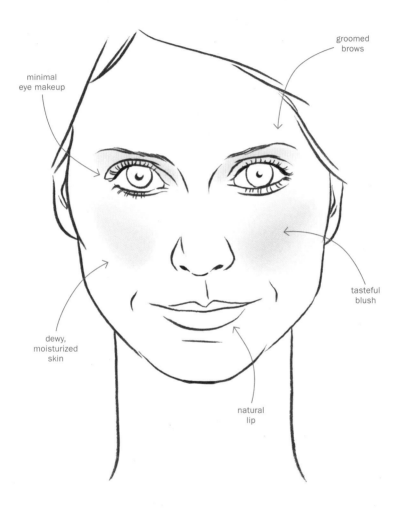

groomed
brows

minimal
eye makeup

tasteful
blush

dewy,
moisturized
skin

natural
lip

SKIN Some people have little to no interest in skincare, while others hoard serums the way that Aidan hoards half-empty deodorants. But no matter where you stand, you must use a cleanser, a toner, an exfoliant, a moisturizer, *and* a sunscreen. Do NOT drop the ball when it comes to sunscreen; it is the closest thing to a fountain of youth that we have.

BROWS The brows of the *Sex and the City* era were pencil thin, and this may or may not be a good look for you. Generally speaking, a natural brow is better suited for a Miranda of the modern era. Tweeze the strays, brush the brow with a spoolie brush, then find a good tinted brow gel to hold the hairs in place.

LIPS Lipstick is optional, but lip balm is not, especially if your skin is routinely ravaged by East Coast winters. If you need a little more oomph, tinted balms and sheer lipsticks are a Miranda's best friend. You don't have to bother with lip pencils and you won't look freakish if you don't have time for a touch-up.

CHEEKS Blush is also optional, but a little bit can go a long way for a Miranda who is tired, stressed, or vitamin D–deficient. As always, less is more. The goal is to look healthy and well-rested, not like the clown at Brady's birthday party.

EYES A good mascara is crucial. However, everyone has wildly different preferences when it comes to both formulas and brushes. You'll have to try a few shitty mascaras before you find one that you actually like. Don't get discouraged by the hunt.

Red Hair, Don't Care

THE MIRANDA'S GUIDE TO HAIR

Mirandas don't just get fucked in the bedroom—they get fucked in the hair salon, too. Yes, everyone has had a bad haircut or a bad hair day, but for Mirandas, a bad hair day can consume years, even decades of their lives. Like dating, finding a preferred hairstyle involves a great deal of trial and error. While not as devastating or permanent as say, a bad tattoo, a terrible coif is no less scarring. Even when you do land on a good style, transitioning it into the next hair phase can be equally fraught. You may have the bone structure for a pixie cut, but you may lack the emotional stamina to grow it into a shoulder-length bob. If your hair is a work-in-progress, don't be disheartened. Bad hair should be celebrated! Like other regrettable decisions in our lives, terrible hairstyles serve as markers for where we've been and where we never want to go again. They build character and provide us with hilarious #TBT material once a comfortable amount of time has passed. So, don't despair if your coked-up hairstylist actively chooses to ignore all of your reference images. Instead, rejoice at another lesson learned. After all, it's just hair. It will grow back. In the meantime, there's a bucket hat that you'll look great in.

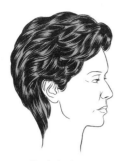

The Androgynous
Bouffant

The Power Lesbian

The Rom-Com Bob

The "I Need to Speak
with the Manager"

The Ducktail

The Businesswoman
Special

Mum's the Word

Few life decisions are more major than the decision to start a family. Some Mirandas intrinsically know that they want kids, while others reach that conclusion after years of skepticism—and of course, many of us have no interest in children at all. In truly epic form, Miranda Hobbes decided to start her family in the lobby of an abortion clinic. Even though a pregnancy was not part of her plan, she threw caution to the wind and decided to raise a baby on her own. It was a badass move, not to mention a refreshing alternative to the white-picket-fence scenario that Charlottes glorify. Her choice was surprising, because our people are not known for their outsize maternal instincts. Many of us don't want children, and the rest of us think that condoms are an acceptable baby shower gift. But regardless of the path that you ultimately choose, you will approach the topic of procreation with the same cynical certainty you bring to every other area of your life. So go forth and multiply. Or just get your tubes tied.

You Want Kids

"I don't like any children but my own."

Congratulations! You're having a baby. Whether this bundle of joy was planned or a total accident, you are now responsible for another human being for the next eighteen years. Because of your pragmatic nature, you are acutely aware of the harrowing realities of motherhood. Despite the financial strain, inevitable sleep deprivation, and the current state of the world—you *still* want to bring a child into it, if for no other reason than to counteract all of the idiots that you see procreating. This is the one realm in a Miranda's life where logic has little bearing. But even though you've decided to have a child, that doesn't mean that you have to buy a cupcake-print apron and do your best Charlotte impersonation for the next two decades. Miranda Hobbes believed that motherhood was a cult (and it is) and she refused to be indoctrinated. Bows, storks, and three-tiered diaper cakes are not an integral part of the experience for you, so if Mommy culture rubs you the wrong way, don't fret. You are free to raise your offspring however you like. Who knows? You might just wind up with another little Miranda.

You Don't Want Kids

"I'm so sick of people with children, they're everywhere!"

Congratulations! You're not having kids. You've made an important decision that flies in the face of society's expectations. You have enough self-awareness to know that you are not the type of person who should care for children in a full-time capacity. Maybe you have a job or a relationship that you'd prefer to focus on, or perhaps you never felt any attachment to children at all. This doesn't make you a monster—after all, the world is positively brimming with Charlottes who are desperate to become mothers. You have other dreams for yourself, and those dreams do not involve bouncy chairs, tantrums, and Minions. You will also get to enjoy the numerous perks of remaining childless, like looking ten years younger than your peers and not having to ruin your living room with an assortment of brightly colored toys. You'll save hundreds of thousands of dollars and the environment will benefit as well. After all, the last thing that this overpopulated planet needs is another little consumer! And while failing to procreate may increase your risk of dying alone and being eaten by your cat, that's a small price to pay for a life lived on your own terms.

Give Back
to the Fucking World

BECAUSE APATHY IS SO LAST SEASON

Altruism *seems* optional, but it's actually a necessary component of a healthy, balanced existence. If you're someone who has strongly held beliefs or sees injustice in the world, it is your obligation to take actions that support those convictions. Making decisions that benefit people beyond yourself doesn't just make the world a better place, it gives you a shot at happiness, because true joy is not attainable to those who are living a life that is out of sync with their fundamental values. No one tells you this, but apathy isn't just destructive to society at large, it's *self-destructive.* A narcissistic existence will slowly rob you of your integrity and self-worth, much like an affair with a married ex. So, if you have a void that cannot be filled with sex, shopping, or Cosmopolitans, it's time to consider giving back to the fucking world.

Every person has a unique skill that can be used for the greater good. Charlotte used her extensive knowledge of modern art to land a docent gig at MoMA. Samantha applied her PR skills to plan a cancer research benefit. Carrie used her writing to connect with

WE SHOULD ALL BE MIRANDAS

disenchanted single women who found solace in her column. While we like to think that Miranda took on the occasional pro-bono case, her willingness to give Steve's mother a sponge bath proved that she was capable of acting beyond her own self-interests. Miranda's selfless action also serves as a reminder that sometimes the best way to give back is to provide support to people in your immediate vicinity. Donating your time or your money to a nonprofit organization is great, but small deeds in your everyday life are just as important. Charitable acts can take on many forms, so don't feel pressured to get on that Friar-Fuck-feeding-the-homeless level straight out of the gate.

__WHAT YOU SHOULD HAVE__
__LEARNED FROM THIS CHAPTER__

- Step away from your smartphone.
- Children are optional, but sunscreen is not.
- Bad hair days build character.
- Reclaim the Cosmopolitan.
- Altruism is self-care.
- Don't eat healthy *all* the time.
- The key to exercise is not hating it.
- Spirituality isn't just for Charlottes.
- Your happiness is your responsibility.
- Your real soulmates are your friends.

THRIVE LIKE A MIRANDA

Are You There Miranda?
It's Me, Carrie

As I laid face-down on the runway in a pair of jewel-encrusted panties, I couldn't help but wonder: is being an It girl really all it's cracked up to be? Getting photographed in the right outfits at the right parties is fun and all, but is an enviable life really more valuable than a stable one? I hate to admit it, but I've always shunned Miranda's pragmatism. After all, if I didn't max out my AmEx from time to time, I wouldn't have such an impressive Dior saddle bag collection today. But after years spent chasing happiness in the form of emotionally unavailable men and Chloé ankle boots, my morale (and my credit score) was at an all-time low. I got to thinking: did my flame-haired friend have the right idea all along? Delayed gratification is boring, but if Miranda's brownstone is any indication— it pays off. As an It girl of a certain age with no plans to plummet out a window, perhaps it's time for me to evolve. Changing my ways won't be easy, but neither is being a senior citizen with an oven full of shoes. In order to survive, I must step out of my comfort zone, even if that means venturing below 23rd Street. I may not know what the future holds, but I know that I'm capable of making better decisions *today*. So when it comes to matters of self-preservation, shouldn't we all be Mirandas?

How do you know when enough is enough?

Y ou may never have a wardrobe like Carrie, a perfect marriage like Charlotte, or a glamorous job like Samantha, but right now, at this very moment: you are enough. Our status-obsessed culture encourages us to strive for things that we cannot attain, to compare ourselves to people who we can never be. We convince ourselves that all of our problems would dissipate if we had the right relationship or the right Gucci handbag, but no amount of outward success can satisfy someone who is always yearning for more.

Mirandas often make the grave mistake of conflating our hopes and ambitions with who we are as people. We closely identify with our goals, and suffer greatly when things don't go according to plan. Many of us feel like we've fallen behind in life, and that we can't possibly feel whole until we accomplish everything that we set out to do—but even the most successful among us often feel an underlying sense of unease. Why? Because our yearnings can never be satiated. When we finally cross something off our list, we may feel a momentary sense of relief, but that relief often gives way to the desire for newness. If we could only get that promotion, or that prewar penthouse, then we could finally relax. But the joke is on us, because this vicious cycle never ends, so if you should find yourself draped in Versace couture at the Hôtel Plaza Athénée and you're still miserable, it may be time to rethink your priorities.

Real happiness comes from our ability to be compassionate toward ourselves and others. It's not a particularly sexy concept, but it's no less true. Making peace with our own shortcomings and treating ourselves with the respect that we reserve for our closest friends is the only path to fulfillment. That said, self-love is no easy task for the Miranda-identified. Not a day goes by when we don't obsess about something that we're lacking, whether it's a relationship, or a high-paying job, or Sarah Jessica Parker's abs. But just because we've struggled with negative thoughts in the past does not mean that we're doomed to hold on to them for life. Simply having awareness of the thoughts as they come is the first step to eradicating them. Many of us suffer from the delusion that the voice in our head speaks the absolute truth. What she says, we believe without hesitation—but might we remind you that this is the same crazy bitch who told you to buy a trucker hat in 2004? It stands to reason that she's wrong about a lot of things.

Self-actualization is not about succeeding on someone else's terms. It is about knowing who you are, and thriving within those parameters. A Miranda can never be a Carrie, no matter how many giant rosettes she buys. If you truly want to be happy, you have to believe that you are enough, right now. Your ability to love yourself cannot be contingent on an abstract future scenario where you're wealthy, married, and twenty pounds lighter. You may have a bad haircut, bad credit, or a brand-new pair of adult braces, but that shouldn't preclude you from the most exciting, challenging, and significant relationship of all: the relationship that you have with yourself. The next time that you find yourself dousing your dessert with dish soap, have a little compassion. You're a Miranda, such humiliations are inevitable, and if you can find someone who will check you into the Betty Crocker Clinic without judgment, well, that's just fabulous.

Acknowledgments

Chelsea and Lauren would like to thank . . .

First and foremost, we must pay respect to our queen, Candace Bushnell. Thank you for committing years of Manhattan nightlife to paper, without which none of this would be possible. To Darren Star, who brought Carrie & Co. to life. And to our second father Michael Patrick King, for your brilliant vision.

To Cynthia Nixon, for inspiring us on-screen and off. You are a true icon, and every Miranda owes you a debt of gratitude. We could not have written this book without you.

To Sarah Jessica Parker, Kristin Davis, and Kim Cattrall, you embodied these characters like no one else could, and we are forever grateful. And to Kristen Johnston, for your truly iconic season six cameo.

To the brilliant Patricia Field, who inspired us to buy giant rosettes circa 2001.

To the angelic writers who have given us so much brilliant material to satirize: Jenny Bicks, Cindy Chupack, and Liz Tuccillo. As well as Julie Rottenberg, Elisa Zuritsky, Amy Harris, Nicole Avril, Allan Heinberg, Terri Minsky, Michael Green, Jenji Kohan, Sue Kolinsky, Ollie Levy, Merrill Markoe, Becky Hartman Edwards, Jessica Bendinger, Alexa Junge, Judy Toll, and Aury Wallington.

To HBO, for never sending us a cease and desist order. Also, please keep us in mind for any and all *Sex and the City* copywriting needs. Additionally, Warner Brothers, feel free to slide into our DMs as we have some ideas for a third *Sex and the City* film (with or without Kim Cattrall).

To our incredible illustrator, Carly Jean Andrews, who absolutely killed it and dealt with all of our annoying emails along the way.

To Google Docs and FaceTime, without which we wouldn't have been able to write this book on two different continents.

To all of our SATC-obsessed friends and collaborators who we have met on this journey. Our agent, Ross Harris, who believed in us from the beginning. Our iconic editor, Kate Napolitano, who was our cheerleader and confidant throughout this process. To these internet strangers who have since become our friends, Dan Clay, Brian Lobel, Justin Teodoro, John Early, Ariella Starkman, Kate Jinx, Claire Roudabush, Stephanie Gonot, Maya Bookbinder, Amy Taylor, and the magical humans at The Standard, Hollywood.

Chelsea would like to thank ...

My fabulous parents, Ben Fairless and Wendy Rowan, for always supporting me. My beautiful wife, Tatiana Waterford, for loving me and putting up with all my bullshit. Clare Adams, for being the sister that I never had. Lea DeLaria, for always believing in me. The Waterfords, for taking such good care of me while I wrote this book. And all my friends in New York City, who I miss so much.

Lauren would like to thank ...

My mother and father, Cathy and Andy Garroni, for loving me, supporting me, and giving me unrestricted access to cable television as a child. Danielle Smith, who has willingly listened to my pop cultural rantings for more than two decades. Jessica Glasscock, who nurtured my love of fashion. And Kayla Harvey, Loren Kramar, and Kailey Marsh for their support and notes throughout this process.